W9-BKF-240

FIND IT
BUY IT
FIX IT

THIRD EDITION

THE INSIDER'S GUIDE TO
FIXER-UPPERS

ROBERT IRWIN

KAPLAN PUBLISHING

SCHAUMBURG TOWNSHIP DISTRICT LIBRARY
130 SOUTH ROSELLE ROAD
SCHAUMBURG, ILLINOIS 60193

643.12
IRWiN, R

3 1257 01706 3461

This publication is designed to provide accurate and authoritative information in regard to the subject matter covered. It is sold with the understanding that the author and the publisher are not engaged in rendering legal, accounting, investment, or other professional service. If legal advice or other expert assistance is required, the services of a competent professional should be sought.

President, Kaplan Publishing: Roy Lipner
Vice President and Publisher: Maureen McMahon
Senior Acquisitions Editor: Vicki Smith
Development Editor: Trey Thoelcke
Production Editor: Karen Goodfriend
Typesetter: Leah Strauss
Cover Designer: Gail Chandler

© 2006 by Robert Irwin

Published by Kaplan Publishing,
a division of Kaplan, Inc.

All rights reserved. The text of this publication, or any part thereof, may not be reproduced in any manner whatsoever without written permission from the publisher.

Printed in the United States of America

06 07 08 10 9 8 7 6 5 4 3 2 1

Library of Congress Cataloging-in-Publication Data

Irwin, Robert, 1941–
Find it, buy it, fix it / Robert Irwin.—3rd ed.
    p. cm.
ISBN-13: 978-1-4195-3572-7
ISBN-10: 1-4195-3572-2
1. House buying. 2. Dwellings—Remodeling. 3. Real estate investment. I. Title.
HD1379.I643 2006
643'.12—dc22

2006011592

Kaplan Publishing books are available at special quantity discounts to use for sales promotions, employee premiums, or educational purposes. Please call our Special Sales Department to order or for more information at 800-621-9621, ext. 4444, e-mail *kaplanpubsales@kaplan*.com, or write to Kaplan Publishing, 30 South Wacker Drive, Suite 2500, Chicago, IL 60606-7481.

Contents

Find It!

1 Profits in Fixers

Do you want to make tens (perhaps hundreds) of thousands of dollars on your next real estate investment?

Do you want to buy into a neighborhood or a house you couldn't otherwise afford?

Do you want to put some "sweat equity" into a property and have a lot of fun doing it?

Do you want to buy a home, fix it up, sell for a profit, and do it again and again, moving up to ever bigger, grander, and more expensive homes?

If you answered yes to any one of these questions (and especially if you answered yes to all of them), then you should try a "fixer." For thousands of Americans, a fixer is the swiftest, surest, and most profitable road to real estate riches.

What Is a Fixer?

Also called a "fixer upper" or a "handyman special," a fixer is a property with a problem. When you buy a brand new property, presumably it's ready to go—just move in and enjoy. For most resales, the fix-up, clean-up, rehab work has already been done by the seller (and added to the price). In both cases, you buy a finished home. However, with a fixer, by definition something always needs to be fixed or improved. You do that work, and you reap the profits.

The easiest example is what I call a "cosmetic fixer." (See Chapter 4.) A cosmetic fixer is discounted because it needs paint; has broken windows, screens, and doors; torn carpeting; and so on. You buy low, do the fix-up work, and sell high. You've become an entrepreneur, an investor . . . a fixer. (The term fixer can be applied both to the properties and to the person who fixes them up.)

What Is Not a Fixer

Obviously, not every house is a fixer; indeed most homes aren't. The trouble is that many popular real estate writers have what I think is the wrong idea about what constitutes a fixer.

It's Not Simply Adding Value

The error is the notion that you can buy almost any property and, by being creative and adding value, resell for a profit.

While you can add value to any property, you won't necessarily make a profit on your work. Indeed, in many cases, you can do a lot of rehab work and come out not adding enough value to cover the costs of the work, let alone make a profit.

The reason has to do with what I call the "white elephant" syndrome. Let's look at an example. The Greens bought a home in Los Angeles, California. It was a single-story, three-bedroom, two-bath house in reasonably good condition. They had a vision, however. They dreamed of a two-story house with Roman-style columns in front. They saw it with brickwork facades and a trellised entrance. So they set about remaking the home. Five months later, they had added almost 800 square feet and given it a whole new look.

Everyone who saw it oohed and aahed over its appearance. It was a work of art. The Greens were thrilled, until they put it up for sale. They figured the rehab work had cost them $200,000. They added that to the price they paid plus another $100,000 for their profit and quickly found out that no buyers were interested. Their home was now hugely overpriced for the neighborhood. They were, in effect, asking $300,000 more than neighboring homes were selling for.

Everyone agreed that their home was truly beautiful and certainly showed what it cost to build. But everyone also pointed out that the house was overpriced for the area. It was a white elephant, something that no one would buy at the price being asked.

The approach of just adding value to a property doesn't pay attention to the limits that the neighborhood will set on the real selling price. The cost of the work added won't necessarily fetch a profitable price.

RULE

Always aim to be able to sell for the price the neighborhood will bear. Never overprice yourself by overdoing the improvements.

A Fixer Is Not Just Finding a Bargain

Another approach that some writers promote is just to look for bargain properties. Here the idea is to find a property that you can buy for way under market—a bargain. Then you fix it up and resell for a profit.

Again, it's certainly true that you can make a profit by fixing up and selling a bargain property. However, if the property is truly bargain priced, then you can flip it, reselling without doing any work at all.

Let's look at an example. The Freemans were looking for a home to live in when they stumbled on a bargain in a suburb of Chicago. According to their careful estimates of property values in the area, the home they were interested in should sell for $175,000. However, the seller was asking only $150,000. And she confessed she was desperate to get out. She would consider almost any offer. The home was dilapidated, and certainly a new coat of paint inside and out would help, as would new carpeting and landscaping. So the Freemans offered $100,000 and were astonished when the seller accepted. They had gotten a real bargain.

They bought the home and not only painted it inside and out and carpeted it but also put in new insulation and a heating and air-conditioning system. They put in new double-pane windows. They replaced all the doors. In effect, they completely renovated the property. Eventually they sold it for $180,000, making $10,000 profit after paying their fix-up costs.

The error they made is what I call the "overkill syndrome." The Freemans were so intent on fixing up the property, they didn't stand back and realize the obvious. They had bought at a tremendous bargain price. For a few thousand dollars in cosmetic renovation (paint and carpeting), they could have then turned around and flipped the property, selling it for about $170,000 to $180,000 and pocketing $60,000 or more. They did too much. They didn't have a fixer, they had a flipper. The improvements they made didn't contribute to their profit.

It all comes down to the fact that they were able to buy at a bargain price. If you can buy for well below market value, why bother to fix up the place (outside of the essentials necessary to make the place showable)? Simply turn around, sell at market value, and take your profit.

Bargains Aren't Easy to Find

Buying bargains can be problematic in another way. It can be darned hard to find them. With the huge appreciation in prices since the turn of the century, nearly all sellers are well aware of the market value of their property. Too often, they want more than its market value, not less. You might have to search through and make offers on hundreds of properties before you find one that you could buy as a bargain.

RULE

Always take advantage of a bargain-priced property, *if* you can find one. Just don't confuse it for a fixer upper.

Looking for That One Special Property

As I mentioned, a true fixer is a property with a problem. The problem forces the seller to sell at a discount (not a bargain, because the problem reduces the property's value). The fixer is distinctive, unlike the other properties around it in some way. (Very rarely will you find two properties with identical problems.) It's one of a kind.

The big advantage to you is that you don't need lots of fixer properties to make a living. Presumably there's only one of you (including your spouse and your team), and you only need one property at a time. Unlike a real estate agent who needs dozens of sales to survive, or a large-scale builder who needs a tract of homes, you only need to find that one, unique property—the one with a problem that you can buy for less (because of that problem), fix up, and resell. Because you're not looking for a bargain, you can find a fixer situation in almost any market.

The distinctive property technique holds up all through the fixer process. When I'm working on a house, I look for unique situations both for labor and for materials. Perhaps I need a bathtub. I could go to Home Depot and buy one "off the rack" for $300 to $500 dollars. On the other hand, maybe my local plumbing supply store has one in a slightly unusual color that it will discount. I once bought a $1,000 cast iron tub for $100 because its color was dark brown and no one else wanted it. I then designed the color of the bathroom around the tub—it was charming and helped sell the property.

Usually, you're at a disadvantage when you're the "little guy," the one of a kind. But with fixers, being distinctive is an advantage. You don't need the average or typical property that most buyers want. You need the unique situation. When you find it, you only need to buy it for its current market value (discounted because of its problem), creatively fix the problem, and resell for the market price the neighborhood will bear.

Think you can do that? Hundreds of thousands of successful people, including me, do it all the time.

The Five Most Common Reasons People Want Fixers

#1. It's a Moneymaker

Fixers are to real estate what cars with scratched paint and dented fenders are to auto resales. They are a challenge and, very often, an opportunity.

A fixed-up house will bring top dollar and a quick sale, while a rundown house will bring a lower price and take longer to sell. So why not buy the rundown house, spend some bucks and effort to fix it up, and then quickly resell it for a profit? Why not indeed? The opportunity to make quick money is the most common reason given for looking at fixers.

#2. It's a Step-up House

Often the fixer is a better house than you could afford to buy if it were in perfect condition. You have to live somewhere, so why not spend the next few months or longer living in a fixer, all the while improving it?

Many people do "serial" fixing. They buy one home, fix it up, and sell it. Then they use the profits to buy a bigger and better fixer and repeat the process. Each step of the way, they move into a bigger and grander home.

#3. It's a Step-up Neighborhood

The expression "champagne taste with a beer budget" applies to almost everyone who wants to buy real estate, simply because real estate is so expensive, particularly in the most desirable areas. We know *where* we want to live, but very often we simply can't afford to move into that neighborhood, at least not at market prices.

But, what if you could buy into that dream neighborhood at below-market cost? Far below?

You usually can, if you're willing to accept a fixer. In virtually every neighborhood, there are those properties that, for whatever reason, owners have allowed to run down. They're the messes and the uglies. Because of their problems, they're much less expensive.

You get into that neighborhood for less money, often much less. And, if you supply the labor, you may be able to fix up a handyman's special for only a fraction of your original purchase price. It's a kind of give and take. You give up something to get something you want. You give up the idea of getting a ready-to-go, polished home and settle for a fixer. In exchange, you get to live in the neighborhood you want.

#4. It's a Lot of Fun

Most of us like to putter around, work in the garage, make things. If that fits you, then working on a fixer can be one of the great experiences of your life (assuming you also take to heart the lessons in this book). If you already are handy and experienced, I shouldn't have to say more. You already know the excitement of starting a new, hands-on project. On the other hand, if this is all new to you but you have a hankering to try, then there's no better way to learn than by doing. Buying a fixer lets you jump in with both feet and, as long as you go slowly, lets you learn and earn as you go. I've had some of the best times of my life fixing up houses with my wife. I suspect the same could hold true for you.

#5.   *It's a Way to Move Up through Real Estate*

Many of us are serial investors. That means that we buy a house, move in, and fix it up; sell it; and then do it all again for another more expensive house. Many real estate investors out there who started in $70,000 homes are now living in multimillion dollar mansions. The techniques for doing this aren't hard to learn, and we'll see them as we progress through this book. If you want to move up through real estate, you can't pick a better way to start than with a fixer.

Ready to make your profits in fixers? Then read on . . .

2 Where to Find Fixers in Any Market

With the price of housing high in most areas of the country, some people think that fixers are no longer available—they've been priced out of the market.

Nothing could be further from the truth.

Fixers are available in all markets and in all areas. True, you may need to pay more for them today than just a few years ago. But today the financing is far better than it was a few years ago, making it easier for almost everyone to borrow more money on real estate. In other words, as never before, you can use other people's money to buy your fixer. (See Chapter 9 for hints on cheap financing.)

Additionally, when you sell, you should be able to reap far greater profits. While higher prices may make buying a bit more difficult, they make it possible to sell for more money.

Finding Fixers When the Market's Hot

While recently the real estate market has cooled in most areas, in a few it's still sizzling. If you're in a hot market, finding a fixer presents two distinct problems:

1. When the market is hot and prices are rising, many sellers figure it will be worthwhile to spend the time and money to do the fix-up work themselves. Thus, a significant portion of fixers will be handled directly by the property owners.
2. Sellers want to believe that a hot market means they don't have to discount the problem property. They figure that some fool will come along and pay top dollar for an inferior property, and too often, they're right.

If you're operating in a hot market, your biggest chore is not finding fixer properties—you can still use the techniques outlined below to locate plenty of them. It's convincing sellers to be realistic about pricing. Check into Chapter 10 for techniques for accomplishing this.

Checking the Listings—Working the MLS

Yes, working with an agent is hardly a new suggestion. However, it is often the best place to start. I always talk to agents and brokers in the area. I tell them what I want, and they try to oblige by finding me the right house.

When you're starting out, working with one agent at a time usually turns out best. Let that agent look for you and continue looking until either you find a good property or the agent runs out of steam. When the latter happens, locate another agent and start again.

Keep in mind, however, that not all agents "co-broker" properties. That is, they don't all cooperate with other brokers on the sale of every house. Some they handle exclusively themselves. This is particularly the case with houses that they think will sell quickly. Sometimes a fixer in a good neighborhood is just such a house. What this means is that over time, it's usually a good idea to introduce yourself to many brokers and let them know that if they have a good fixer, you're ready, willing, and able to make a quick purchase decision.

In addition to letting the agent look for you, you should also use the agent's access to the Multiple Listing Service (MLS) to look for yourself. Today, MLS listings are available on the computer. (You can also find most of them yourself at *www.realtor.com.*) By spending a few hours in your agent's office in front of the computer, you should be able to come up with at least half a dozen properties to check out.

Pay particular attention to the following in MLS listings:

- *Keywords.* Words such as *needs love, sweat equity, needs TLC,* and, of course, *fixer.*
- *Stale listings.* These are more than ten weeks old and are getting ready to expire (most listings are for three months.) Often the reason a property doesn't sell quickly is because it needs fixing up. Also, as time goes by, the seller gets increasingly anxious to sell and becomes more willing to offer a discount.
- *Pictures.* Often a picture of the property is shown. Many times, the picture says far more than words about the home's condition. Look for homes that look run down.
- *Odd properties.* After a while, you should be able to recognize homes by neighborhood. Sometimes a home will stand out— bigger, smaller, taller, more/less land, and so forth. The oddness of the property may mean that it's got a problem worth fixing.
- *Defined problem.* Sometimes the problem is laid out for you— the house is slipping down the hill, there's a bad roof or foundation, ground water issues exist, and so on. These may be spelled out right on the listing.
- *Zoning issues.* Usually these involve such problems as having a multiple-use property on land zoned for single use, for example, a property being rented out as a boarding house on land zoned only for single-family usage. Get the property at a discounted price, fix the zoning issue (when possible), and reap the profits.
- *Neighborhood issues.* These are almost never spelled out in the listing. You have to know the neighborhoods well enough to recognize when they produce problems for a house. Get the home at a discount and then help fix up the neighborhood. You sometimes can do this, but it takes time.

- *Expireds.* Listings whose time has run out with the agent are also available. Often other agents comb through these trying to relist them. You can check these to see if the reason they didn't sell is because they had a fixer problem. Usually you'll need an agent who trusts you to buy through them to be shown these.

Look at FSBOs

These are properties offered For Sale By Owner (FSBO). While they are not listed, they are available directly from the seller, and often that seller will be happy to pay at least half a commission to your agent for handling the deal with you. Of course, you could collect half yourself by buying direct and eliminating the agent. See my book, *For Sale by Owner Kit* (Kaplan Publishing), for more information.

You can find FSBOs three ways:

1. You can walk/drive the neighborhoods looking for "By Owner" signs. I drive all the streets in the neighborhood(s) I'm interested in as often as possible. I look for FSBO signs as well as obviously rundown properties. I call the FSBOs and find out if the property may be a fixer opportunity. I leave a business card (or note) on the rundown houses asking the owners to contact me if they want to sell.
2. You can check out the paper for ads that say FSBO or "By Owner."
3. And you can look on the Internet for FSBO Web sites such as:
   - Owners.com
   - FSBO.com
   - Forsalebyowner.com
   - Byowner.com

The big problem with FSBOs is not finding those that are fixers, but rather finding sellers who don't have an inflated idea of what their property is worth. Too often sellers list their property as a FSBO because they don't want to listen to what an agent tells them is the right market price—they want more.

Check Advertising

I read all the local papers, including throwaways and weeklies, that advertise property for sale. You never know where someone will advertise. Look for the small, two- and three-line ads. Often that's where the fixers show up.

I also stop at the local grocery stores and pharmacies to check their bulletin boards. A seller with a fixer problem will often pin up a notice asking for buyers.

Check Older Areas

The age of a neighborhood is a definite factor in determining whether and how many fixers will be in it. The older the area, the more likely it has fixers. Most cities in the United States have developed outward from a central core. First came the original development, perhaps at the turn of the last century or earlier. Then came the suburbs, often spreading out during the 1940s, 1950s, and 1960s. And then, more recently, came the far suburbs, located miles from the old central city, which often became their own complete cities.

If you were to plot the typical metropolitan area's growth graphically, it might look something like Figure 2.1.

FIGURE 2.1

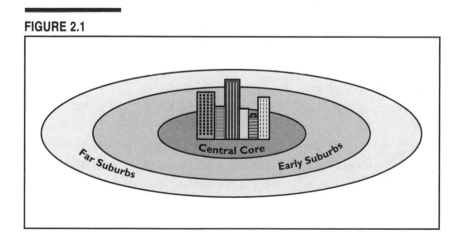

HINT

Older areas, particularly those that have aged well and are still popular, are happy hunting grounds for fixers.

Check Out the Inner City

All across the country, major cities are revitalizing their central core. Old commercial buildings are becoming condos and offices or are coming down to make way for new shopping malls. Theater districts are being rejuvenated. Even slums are being cleared out for new highrise dwellings and high-tech office centers.

Central city revitalization presents an opportunity for you. With exciting new core areas often offering new job opportunities, many people are now moving back to the city. They are looking to purchase good homes in up-and-coming areas.

As a result, many older, rundown residential blocks are seeing new life, with home after home being fixed up and resold. The trick is to find the right neighborhood at the right time. If you do, you may be able to buy cheap, fix up, and resell for a hefty profit.

The "right neighborhood" often means an older, often blighted, area that has already started to turn upward. Every block will have several fixed-up homes, often right next to dilapidated buildings. Find one of these areas. Buy a rundown house at a low price.

After you fix it up, you can ride the wave of neighborhood rejuvenation to profits.

Beware, however, of buying too early, before a neighborhood turns around. The temptation here is great, because the houses in these yet to be discovered areas will be the cheapest. However, some neighborhoods, because of gangs, vandalism, or a poor location with regard to where the core action is, may take longer to rejuvenate. Some neighborhoods simply get skipped over by the new activity.

Don't be pennywise and pound foolish looking for the very cheapest home. Buy in a neighborhood where visible redevelopment is taking place at a hectic rate. You'll pay more, but you'll profit more from being in a real turnaround situation.

Check the Early Suburbs

The early suburbs are now the aging suburbs. The homes built there are now reaching the middle to end of their life span at 40 to 50 years. This is where most people look. However, it's not the best place to find good fixers.

In many areas, older suburbs in many areas are now rapidly becoming the new slums.

As a result, many fixers appear to exist in the early suburbs. However, the very fact that there are so many often works against their potential profitability. A very important rule of real estate is to remember that, while you can do wonders for an individual property, by yourself it's difficult to help a neighborhood. Nothing's worse than to buy a house; put time, money, and sweat into it; and then not be able to resell because the neighborhood is so bad.

On the other hand, if you're entrepreneurial and philanthropically minded, you could devote time and energy to organizing and revitalizing the neighborhood. One determined person can do amazing things. And at the end of the rainbow is a pot of gold; turn the neighborhood around, and your property will skyrocket in value.

My suggestion is that, if you're interested in purchasing in an early suburb (defined as a neighborhood where the houses are between 35 and 50 years old), you pay extra special attention to the homes surrounding your potential fixer. Check out the surrounding blocks. If the houses have been largely kept up, if lawns and gardens look good, if there's a sense of well-being and security, then you've found a pocket where buying a fixer can make great sense.

On the other hand, if the yards are rundown, the houses neglected, and a feeling of danger and crime pervades the area, you'd be wasting your money trying to fix up such a place.

RULE

No matter how much money, time, and effort you spend (and sometimes you can spend too much), you *alone* can never overcome a bad neighborhood.

Look Closely at the Far Suburbs

Beginning in the early 1970s, people moved even farther away from the central city. Their goal was cheap housing, safe neighborhoods, and good schools. The distance from the central city became huge, sometimes 40 to 50 miles or more away. Sometimes these far suburbs became their own smaller cities.

Today these far suburbs usually contain the newest homes and sometimes the most upscale neighborhoods. They may have gated communities, wide streets, and parks with walking trails. Crime rates tend to be lower. Because of their newness, finding a fixer here usually means locating a house with an environmental, geological, or structural problem. Unfortunately, these can be the most difficult to correct.

Also, when looking for a fixer in a far suburb, you must be particularly careful to make a clearheaded judgment about the neighborhood. No longer can you simply think that in a distant suburb, prices and demand will continually increase. In some such areas, the trend is now the other direction. Before even looking for fixers, you want to be sure the area is still desirable. Check with local brokers who can give you recent median sales prices for various neighborhoods. You're looking for a steady upward trend. Also, check out employment opportunities with the local chamber of commerce. You want to invest in an area that offers lots of jobs.

Consider Custom Homes

Given the choice of getting a fixer in a tract or in a custom area (all else being equal), go with the custom area every time. The reason is the property's potential.

In a tract area, you can never do more to a house than bring it back to its former state. In real estate, regardless of what some experts claim, value is still determined by what similar properties recently sold for. A tract house is likely to have a dozen comparables that sold over the last year. As a result, its price is locked. Everything you do to the place to make it better than its cousins will be considered overfixing or creating a white elephant. (See Chapter 1.) Consequently, you won't be able to multiply your profits.

RULE

Value is not based on how much money you spend fixing up a place or how much time and effort you spend working on it. Remember, no one wants to get stuck with an overbuilt property.

The big advantage of buying in an area of custom homes is that no exact comparable properties exist. Here you may have a house of 1,500 square feet next to one of 3,000 square feet. You will have all types of architectural designs, lot sizes, and landscaping.

As a result, selling price limitations become less of a problem. Appraisers will often look for comparables on the basis of square footage or similar locations.

In short, you have the opportunity here to be more creative with what and how you fix up, at the same time still having a good chance of being able to realize a profit. Plan your fixer to sell in the midrange of the area's sold properties for a faster sale.

Looking at Foreclosures and REOs

Here you're looking at property with two problems. One is that it's in foreclosure or is Real Estate Owned (REO). An REO is a property taken back through foreclosure and now being sold by a lender. The other is that it may be a fixer. Sometimes real opportunities abound in foreclosures and REOs. We'll cover them in detail in Chapter 3.

Other Property Types

Thus far, we've been exclusively discussing houses. However, you can work with other types of fixers. For example, if you're looking for a bigger challenge, you may want to buy a fixer apartment building, industrial building, small commercial strip, or condo or co-op. Many times, these other property types offer greater opportunities than houses for fixing, especially if you can then hold them as a longer-term investments until a selling opportunity occurs.

Apartment Buildings

I've tackled this type of fixer, and I can assure you it's a real challenge. Whatever you would do in a house, you have to do many times over. The problems escalate as the number of units increase. Even a four-unit building can be a full-time job when it comes to fixing up. After all, you have to fix up four times as many kitchens, baths, bedrooms, etc. On the other hand, when you're done, you tend to make four times as much money.

What should you watch out for when buying to fix up?

Dangerous neighborhoods. Don't buy in an area where you'd be afraid to go at night to collect the rent.

Structural problems. With a house, only one unit is empty. With an apartment building, you could be losing rent on all units while fixing the structure.

Low occupancy areas. Remember, an apartment building is a business. If not enough tenants are around to fill it, regardless of how good a fixer candidate it is, you'll eventually lose money.

Industrial Buildings

There are relatively few fixer opportunities in industrial buildings, because in most cases, the structure is just a shell with tenants making improvements. However, occasionally a whole industrial area will be run down, resulting in a low occupancy rate.

The key to success is to find the kind of tenant who wants this building, then fix it up to suit the tenant. An example is changing usage, such as taking a large industrial building in an area with a need for office space and converting it into many small office suites.

Commercial Strip

Usually opportunities in commercial strips come about because the owners have let the properties run down to the point where they can't get high-paying commercial tenants. Because the selling price is based on the strip's income, you can often get these run down strips for a song.

The trick is to fix them up to the point where a strong tenant will want to move in. Once you have one strong tenant, others will follow, and eventually you'll have high rents and be able to sell for a profit.

Condos and Co-ops

Generally speaking, the only type of condo or co-op fixer you should consider is one that only requires a cosmetic fix. When you purchase a shared ownership type of property, the only part of the property that you really control is inside your living area. The roof, outside walls, foundation, structure, and so on are all owned in common and administered through the homeowners' association (HOA). Therefore, any damage or problems must be handled through the HOA.

As a result, you won't want any condos or co-op fixers with serious problems. You won't be able to control the fixing process, or even if it gets done. Paint, cleanups, and fixture repair or replacement you can handle. While this can knock the price down a bit, it's unlikely to create the deep price discounts that you'll find in the other types of fixers.

3 Fixers in Foreclosure

Sometimes the best fixers to be found are in foreclosure. Often a serious problem is causing the old owner to give up on the property, letting it go back to the lender. As a result, you may be able to buy it for a deep discount.

If you buy a fixer directly from a seller while it's in foreclosure (a tricky business, as we'll shortly see), you sometimes can get it for just the existing financing, if the owner is willing just to get out from under it. Of course, many times these properties are "upside down," meaning that the seller owes more than it's worth, and in those situations you're better off passing. An exception would be if you can negotiate with the lender for a "short sale," where the lender accepts less than the loan amount.

On the other hand, you can also buy an REO (real estate owned) directly from a lender. yThis is a fixer that the lender has taken back from a borrower and now owns. Now the lender has double trouble on its hands—it has a liability (the property) as well as a fixer. Take both problems off the lender's hands, and you can often get a terrific discount.

Foreclosure offers unusual challenges as well as opportunities for the person looking for a fixer upper.

What Is Foreclosure?

payments. The time required for the process itself varies from state to state, from only a few months to as much as a year. The original borrower continues to own the property until the foreclosure process is complete and title transfers to the lender. During this time, borrowers are almost always desperately trying to sell to get out from under the foreclosure to preserve their credit record and perhaps to recoup a few dollars.

Usually during the early days of the foreclosure process, the borrower will try to keep up the property when there's still hope of getting a sale. But, as the foreclosure deadline draws closer, typically the borrower lets the property run down. Remember, sometimes a foreclosure will take a year or longer to conclude.

If the seller can't afford the mortgage payments, chances are they can't afford upkeep costs. Further, many foreclosed borrowers resent the entire process. They feel that no matter the circumstances (and often the foreclosure results because of circumstances beyond their control, such as illness in the family, job loss, and so on), it's their house and they shouldn't be forced out. Sometimes they will express their anger in a backlash against the lender. Hence, houses that are taken back will sometimes have moderate to severe damage, including holes in walls, broken windows, broken toilets and sinks, damaged furnace/air conditioners, and so on. Of course, as we've learned in the last chapter, all of these are cosmetic damages.

Added Risk When Buying Directly from the Seller in Foreclosure

If you deal directly with a seller who is in foreclosure, you carry more risks than if you were to buy the property at an arm's length sale. For one, you run the risk of that seller coming back at a later time and claiming that you used undue influence to lower the price. Some states allow such sellers to reclaim their property.

Check with an attorney in your area to see what rights are available to a seller from whom you want to buy a property in foreclosure.

Further, you often must deal not only with the seller but with the lender. The lender will always add in back payments, including interest and penalties. As a consequence, the price to get the house out of foreclosure and purchase it may be higher than the seller initially realizes. You may end up wasting a lot of time thinking you could buy at one price, only to find that the purchase price is much higher—too high for you to buy, fix up, and make a profit on the property. And more than one lender may be involved.

CAUTION

The seller of a house in foreclosure may have a long-term right of redemption (buy-back).

Added Opportunity

On the other hand, you may have leverage with the lender of a property in foreclosure. Particularly in a real estate market with a lot of foreclosures, you may be able to work out a deal whereby the lender forgoes certain interest amounts and penalties, sometimes even principal, to get rid of the mortgage. This is called a "short sale."

Of course, no lender will come to you with such an offer. You must negotiate it yourself. If you find yourself in such a position, I suggest you read my book *Tips and Traps for Negotiating Better Real Estate Deals* (McGraw-Hill, 2005).

Better Opportunities in REOs?

A lender, who is in the business of making loans and not owning property, usually wants to get rid of real estate as soon as possible. REOs initially are almost always fixers. Lenders, however, are not stupid (no matter how crazy their lending policies may sometimes seem), and they will make a decision about an REO. Either they will fix it up themselves, in which case it's no longer of interest to us because it will not be discounted, or they will sell it "as is," in which case we're very much interested.

REOs do exist in almost every market. For a wide variety of reasons, people here and there are always losing their properties to foreclosure, and lenders are forced to take them back. Lenders desperately want to get rid of REOs as soon as possible. REOs show up on a lender's books as liabilities instead of assets. A lender with too many REOs may be closed down by the government for insolvency. Therefore, if you can contact a lender at just the right time, you may be able to help the lender (and yourself) by taking an REO off its books.

Is an REO a Bargain?

A bargain is a property that you can buy below market and then quickly flip. REOs usually aren't bargains in this sense. The reason is simple: If the property can be quickly flipped, the lender will do it and not sell it to you.

However, taking into account the work to be done, lenders will frequently cut the price of the property. They'll be willing to sell it to you for a price that will allow you to do the required fix-up work and then sell for a healthy profit. No, they're not usually bargains, but usually they are deeply discounted.

Keep in mind, however, that lenders are tough negotiators. If you come in with a low-ball offer (discussed in Part Two), you may not get an immediate response. The lender may simply say it will "think about it." Remember, the lender is on the hook for the value of the mortgage that was on the property. It's not going to be eager to take a loss, unless it feels there's no possibility of other offers. The lender may simply stall you, hoping someone will come in with a higher offer.

Because they are in the business, lenders know pretty closely what a house is worth in any given condition, and they're always trying to realize a profit for themselves. The great danger, therefore, is that because it's an REO, you may think it's a better deal than it really is. Remember, most REOs are discounted but are not bargains.

A few years ago I bought an REO that was in terrible condition. I got it for about a third less than market price for a similar home in good shape and thought I had done well. But by the time I fixed up all its problems and resold it, I barely got my investment in time and money back, let alone made a profit. It was an expensive lesson.

HINT

REOs may offer great opportunities, or they may be money pits. Be careful; take a long look before you buy an REO. Get a thorough property inspection.

What about Government REOs?

In many areas of the country, the government—through the Federal Housing Administration (FHA) or veterans programs— will offer REOs for sale. These are homes taken back through fore-closure by lenders and then assumed by a government agency as part of its insurance or guarantee to the lender. Most of these homes are in terrible shape. The government will fix up some before offering them for sale. Forget about these fixed-up proper-ties. Although the prices asked are often slightly below market, these homes do not offer a fix-up opportunity or an opportunity for flipping.

Others, however, the government will offer "as is." I've found some of these to be real opportunities. Although the damage is usually what we've defined as cosmetic, the prices are often rock bottom. If no or few other bidders come forward, you can some-times really get a steal here.

But, again, be careful. Don't get caught up in the bidding and overpay. Set your limit before you start making offers.

A Double-Edged Sword

As I said, foreclosures offer opportunities as well as challenges. Remember that working on fixers can be tantamount to a full-time job. Finding and successfully buying foreclosures at deep discount can also be close to a full-time job. Looking for fixers in foreclosures, therefore, can be like having two full-time jobs.

Yes, you can succeed and do very well. Or you can get caught up wasting a lot of time and energy without seeing positive results. My suggestion is that, if you're just starting out, you take on only one full-time job at a time.

4 What Kind of Fixer Is It?

Some people will walk into a brand new house, look it over, and decide that it's a fixer. Perhaps there's a scratch on the woodwork here, a mark on the sink there, some dust on the windowsill. "The seller should discount this property," they might say, "because of the damage."

Obviously, if it's a brand new property it's not likely to be a fixer. Further, *all*
for will have some defects, even if they're very slight. It's important not to get hung up thinking that if a property isn't perfect it must be a fixer. Fixers are homes with *real* problems.

But what, exactly, constitutes a fixer? How will you recognize one when you see it?

The truth is that fixers come not only in every shape and size but also in every kind of condition. I've identified four basic states that almost all fixer properties fit into. Categorizing your potential purchase into one of these will help you identify not only if it's a fixer but what kind of fixer.

The four main categories are:

1. Cosmetic
2. Rejuvenator
3. Broken-back
4. Scraper

We'll consider each separately.

Cosmetic.

- Bad curb appeal (looks terrible when you drive up)
- Needs paint
- May have broken windows and doors
- Carpet stained and/or torn
- Holes in walls
- May have broken appliances and fixtures

Rejuvenator.

- Hidden problems (often looks better than the cosmetic fixer)
- Needs wall and floor insulation
- Needs new heating/cooling system
- Needs to be replumbed and/or rewired
- Needs termite damage repaired
- Other hidden damage

Broken-back.

- May look good or bad
- Has a seemingly unsolvable problem, such as a cracked foundation, too few bedrooms or bathrooms, or collapsed roof beams
- Damage from earthquake, flood, or other natural catastrophe
- Lead or asbestos contamination

Scraper.

- No foundation
- Violates building codes
- Ready to fall down
- No hope of salvage

What Is a Cosmetic Fixer?

If you've been looking at homes, you'll know this type when you see it. Basically, there's nothing wrong with the structure—it just looks bad. Typically, the paint will be old, stained, dirty, or even peeling. Windows may be cracked. Sinks may be broken or missing. The carpet may be stained or torn. The lawn and shrubbery are dead or dying.

This is the perfect fixer for most people. The worse the place looks, the better. You *want* the front door to be hanging at an angle on broken hinges. You *want* there to be holes in the walls. You *want* the light fixtures to have been stolen with just bare wires hanging from the ceilings.

Why do you want these problems? Because the worse the place looks, the more difficulty the seller will have finding a buyer and the lower the price will be.

Keep two things in mind. First, most sellers with this kind of property realize what the problem is and spend a few thousand dollars making it look better. They can have the whole inside and outside spray painted, some cheap carpeting put in, and fixtures replaced and in a few weeks get tens of thousands more for the better-looking home. But not all sellers are savvy. Some don't have the money, and some just don't care. They will put the house up for sale as is (or let it go to foreclosure, as in Chapter 3). In short, while cosmetic fixers aren't usually abundant in good neighborhoods, they are around if you search.

The second thing to keep in mind is that, as bad as the description I've given of a cosmetic fixer is, everything I've noted is still cosmetic. By this, I mean you can fix it all with paint, plaster, carpeting, and some new fixtures. You or I or any handy person can do it. You don't need the services of a professional plumber or electrician. All that's needed is a little time, a little money, and some design skills (picking colors, textures, and so on).

What Is a Rejuvenator?

A rejuvenator may sometimes look much the same as a cosmetic fixer—most of the time it looks better. Often it's not very run down and may need relatively little paint, plaster, and superficial repair work. What it does need, however, is upgrading that may not show.

The typical rejuvenator is an older home. Specifically, it's older *and* it's obsolete. It may lack insulation and an adequate heating system (by modern standards). The plumbing may leak and be clogged, or the wiring may not handle modern loads (such as required by a clothes washer, dryer, big refrigerator, and computer). Maybe the home has wood floors that have been infested with termites and require removal and replacement. Or perhaps the house is so old-fashioned that it has an outhouse instead of a bathroom. (Don't laugh! Sometimes these "quaint" old places coexist with modern homes for long periods of time before they are discovered by people such as yourself.) In short, time has simply passed by this type of home.

The problem with the rejuvenator is that it's in far worse shape than it looks. Often the owner will turn a deaf ear to arguments that the house needs tens of thousands of dollars in updating when the need isn't obvious. Instead, the owner may try to sell it for what modern homes in the neighborhood are going for. Don't be an unwary buyer who thinks it's just a cosmetic fixer.

An independent home inspection and careful reading of the seller's disclosure statement can keep you from buying a rejuvenator that you think is a cosmetic fixer. If you're lucky, you'll find this home after it's been on the market for a year or so, and you'll be able to get the seller to accept a realistic offer. But then be prepared for not only hard labor but also work that may require the skills (and expense) of professional repair people.

What Is a Broken-Back Fixer?

This type of fixer can be old or new, cosmetically clean or a rat's nest, rejuvenated or decrepit. What sets a broken-back fixer apart is that it has an apparently implacable problem.

What could such a problem be? The broken-back fixer may only have one bathroom and two bedrooms where the minimum for the neighborhood is two bathrooms and three bedrooms. Sometimes a former owner may have tried to add on an extra bathroom and bedroom, only making the place worse with unskilled work.

Other broken-back fixers have a seriously cracked foundation or are on a hillside where the ground is shifting and threatening to destroy the house. The seller may have tried to put on a new, heavier roof, only to have the roof beams collapse. There could be earthquake, hurricane, tornado, or other damage. In short, the house has a big problem that looks impossible to fix. The seller, realizing the difficulty, is willing to let the place go for a fraction of its value were it in good shape.

The key to successfully handling the broken-back fixer is to come up with a creative way of correcting the problem that isn't difficult to do and that doesn't cost a lot of money. Some very creative people have made fortunes solving apparently unsolvable problems with this type of fixer home.

What Is a Scraper?

Finally, we come to the ultimate fixer, a house with no future. I once owned just such a place. It was on a valuable lot, but the home had been built at the turn of the century and didn't have a cement foundation. Instead, it used an older mudsill method. It didn't have conventional walls with a framework onto which exterior and interior sheeting is nailed but just had slats nailed diagonally together. The bathroom was on the back porch. The plumbing was primitive. The electrical system was dangerous. The roof was made of a wild hodgepodge of shingles, tin, and tar paper. I think you get the idea. It was beyond having an "implacable problem." It was hopeless. What to do?

With a scraper, the key is to buy the property very cheaply because of the obvious problem with the house. You buy it so cheaply, in fact, that you can afford to "scrape" it off the lot and start from scratch, building a new home.

What would be the advantage here over, say, simply buying an already built new home or an already empty lot? One advantage is neighborhood. Often these scrapers are in dynamite neighborhoods where no more lots are available. You can buy the property cheaply, then quickly put up a house and sell for a ton of money. It's being done every day in almost every good, older neighborhood around the country.

Also, these homes are usually already connected to sewer and utilities, and because you are rebuilding instead of starting with a virgin lot, it may be a lot simpler to get city and county permits as well as building and planning department permissions.

The key here, as noted, is to get the lot cheap. However, that's often as big a problem as with the other types of fixers, because the seller often sees not just the lot but also the house that's currently on it. Such sellers refuse to see the existing house as a liability—that is, it will cost money to have it scraped off—and instead insist that the house is really an asset.

But you come in; convince the seller to be realistic; put up a finer, bigger, and more modern house (though being careful not to overbuild for the neighborhood); and thus dramatically increase the property's value. In the end, you sell for a profit.

These are the four types of fixer specials you're likely to encounter. We'll have more to say about each of them as we go through this book. But for now, ask yourself which fixer level you can handle.

What Type of Fixer Should You Aim For?

Each of the four fixer types just mentioned will require specific kinds of work. If you're like most who purchase these properties, you'll plan to do much of the work yourself. (We'll have more to say about hiring out jobs in Chapter 15.) After all, one sure way to save money is to do the labor yourself.

At the outset, it's important to understand your own level of skill. What kind of work and how much are you willing to do yourself? What kind of work do you feel is too difficult for you?

It's also important that the type of fixer you buy be a good match for the level of work you want to do. The worst thing that can happen is for you to buy a fixer only to discover that it requires work that's simply too much for you. In this situation, you might have to hire expensive professionals to do the design and planning as well as the actual labor. This could turn an otherwise potentially profitable fixer into a money pit.

RULE

Don't overestimate—or underestimate—your abilities.

To help you judge your skills, here are some clues as to what you might be able to handle given the level of job you think you want to tackle.

Are You a Dabbler?

My wife is a dabbler when it comes to fixers. She actually enjoys doing painting and wallpapering, tasks that I find tedious. And though she might not enjoy it, she's willing to do cleaning if necessary. (You can hire a crew for about $200 to $400 to come in for a day to make an entire house almost spotless.) However, my wife won't touch anything that requires even the simplest electrical or plumbing work. Things such as putting in a new wall switch, installing a new garbage disposal, or hanging a new light fixture she leaves to someone else (me).

Between the two of us, at this level, we are essentially dabblers. We are always on the lookout for another fixer house, but my wife looks primarily at the cosmetics of the place. She understands her limitations and, were it not for me, would never consider any property other than a cosmetic fixer.

If you're a dabbler, be aware that plenty of properties are out there waiting for you. You will be able to buy them at discount and, by doing the work largely yourself, you should be able to resell at a profit. Probably not for as big a profit as if you had taken on some of the other types of fixers, but you won't have strained your pocketbook, your back, or your psyche.

Are You an Enthusiast?

Even though I've taken on all kinds of fixer projects in my time, I'm probably an enthusiast. I like to look at a house's systems. If a heating system needs work, I'll try to figure out how best to fix it. If the house needs to be completely replumbed, I feel confident I can do it.

In more serious cases, I also like the creativity involved in solving a difficult problem. I've worked on houses that were slipping down hillsides (installing new foundations to hold them in place), taken on cracked foundations and slabs (stabilizing these in many different ways), tackled broken roofs, and so on. For me, these tasks are actually fun! I enjoy the challenge of first figuring out a solution and then watching it work.

For me, as for other enthusiasts, the rejuvenator and the broken-back fixers are ideal. I don't see these as problems but as opportunities.

Are You a Builder?

Finally, we come to the builder. This person often is in the building trades and has a contractor's license (although that's not normally necessary for working on your own home). The builder likes to do the job right; that is, from the ground up. This sort of person typically doesn't enjoy going back and remodeling or fixing up. What the builder wants to do is design a home or other property from scratch. Builders want to do the foundation, the walls, the roof, the ceilings—everything.

But, unlike major contractors, they usually don't want to do it full-time. They prefer it be an *avocation* rather than a vocation. As a result, the scraper is ideal for them. Yes, they may take on the other types, but they won't be happy unless they're doing the real thing.

I've done a few buildings from the ground up, and it can be very satisfying to sit back and look at the building that you've created. Remember that the builder also must deal with scheduling, working with material suppliers and subcontractors, fighting city hall over plans, and all the other issues associated with building from scratch. If you fit this mold, then by all means go with what you do best. Besides, you're likely to make the most money from fixers.

How Do You Get the Right Mix?

Following, then, are the four types of houses and the three types of people who get into fixing them up. I've positioned them in their most likely matchups.

Dabbler

Cosmetic.

- Easiest to do for beginner
- Work can be done part-time
- All work can be done by you
- Has least costly repairs of the four types
- Is quickest to fix

Enthusiast

Rejuvenator.

- Requires an advanced beginner, who is ready to face more difficult problems and has already done at least one fixer project, either a cosmetic or a rejuvenator with someone else
- May require professional help
- Hidden problems can lead to costly repairs
- Can often be salvaged with creative fixes

Broken-back.

- Requires an advanced fixer who has successfully completed at least one rejuvenator
- Often requires risky solutions that may cost a lot of money and time and may still not work
- Can turn into a full-time job

Builder

Scraper.

- Experience with construction work required
- Usually a full-time job, even if it's a second job
- If you're not experienced, you have two choices: either do your first scraper with an experienced partner, or take a percentage for finding the property and turn the job over to a pro.

Warning Signs for First-Time Fixers

Look for any of ten red flags when working with fixers. If these crop up during your initial inspection, you should seriously consider buying into another project. Sometimes the way to win is simply not to play.

1. Broken foundation
2. Collapsed roof
3. Shifting soil
4. Major lead or asbestos contamination
5. Leaking galvanized steel pipes
6. Bad wiring
7. Bulging or broken walls
8. Fewer bathrooms or bedrooms than desirable houses or condominiums in that neighborhood or building
9. Extensive termite damage
10. Extensive earthquake, flood, hurricane, etc. damage

5 Getting to the Right Price

How much should you pay for a fixer? Any fixer? There's actually a formula, which we'll get to shortly, that will tell you. But before you can use it, you need to make some realistic calculations as to your total expenses for the project.

Let's say that you've found a fixer that you really like and want to buy. It's got location, it's run down in a way you can repair, and it seems as though the seller is willing to talk a reasonable price. It's got everything going for it. Or does it?

Before you lay down a dollar, you need to ask some very specific questions and get some very specific answers. Here's the basic formula for determining price that all successful fixers use. We'll see how this works through the remainder of this chapter.

Resale price – Total costs & Profit = Purchase price

Introducing Yourself to the Property and Neighborhood

I was interested in a house in an old part of Sacramento in a well-preserved neighborhood. I had checked with agents and knew that properties were easy to sell there, mainly because of the location close to downtown and the nice setting.

The house I found was a two-story Victorian. It had all kinds of gables and railings and other vintage accessories, most in pretty good shape. I had seen these houses modernized, which is a fancy way of saying all their finery had been stripped and a cheap fiberglass roof and aluminum siding had been put on. Houses treated like this usually ended up looking ghastly. I, however, intended to restore this old place to its former grandeur and resell for a bundle in the process.

The property was a combination cosmetic fixer and rejuvenator. It needed painting and dressing up inside and out. But it also needed a new heating/cooling system as well as electrical repairs. And I'd have to move some of the walls to make rooms that would be more appealing to modern buyers. In short, it was a big project.

The seller, Mrs. Smith, was a little old lady who seemed to have trouble hearing and seeing (though I suspected her disabilities were at least partly an act) and who kept wanting to feed me cookies and milk each time I dropped by. The house was listed, but apparently Mrs. Smith had an arrangement with her agent to show the property herself in exchange for paying a reduced commission. That was fine with me.

The asking price was $285,000 as is. The "as is" was to let buyers know that the seller wasn't going to put up any money to fix the place. Presumably Mrs. Smith would disclose any and all problems, but fixing them would be the buyer's task. The price, she said, was about $50,000 less than what comparable homes in first-class shape had sold for. At first glance, it seemed a fixer project made in heaven.

But I knew I had to check it out. First, I verified what comparable homes had sold for. This was fairly easy. I checked with the listing agent as well as another broker. Indeed, other properties reported to be in first-rate condition had sold during the past six months for prices ranging from $305,000 to $350,000. Mrs. Smith hadn't been fibbing about the prices.

Second, I checked out several of these comparables. I simply had my agent call the current owners of homes that had sold, explain that I was planning to buy a comparable home, and ask if I could come by and look at their homes. Out of five calls, three agreed. I went by, knocked on the door, and introduced myself. In all three cases, I was asked in and was shown around the house. Every house had been freshly painted and cleaned and had had its plumbing and electrical systems upgraded. In two homes, the rooms had been enlarged or combined. I confirmed that the resale prices were indeed for fixed-up houses—not fixers.

Third, I had to determine how much it would realistically cost for me to fix up the house. This was a bit harder. I made a list of the items that needed work.

Cosmetic.
- Clean yard and put in lawn and shrubs
- Replaster as needed and repaint inside
- Repaint exterior

Major work.
- New wood roof
- New wood siding on two outside walls
- New heating system
- Upgrade plumbing system, particularly drains and bathrooms
- Upgrade electrical system

When I finished my list and looked at it, I had to whistle in surprise. An amazing amount of work needed to be done.

Can Estimates Save You?

I had done many fixers by then and felt I could give a pretty accurate estimate for most of the items. But this was my first Victorian, so I called up several people with whom I had previously worked: an electrician, a plumber, a heating/air-conditioning person, and a roofer. Because they already knew me, they agreed to come out within the next day or two. What they told me was most revealing.

I should mention that, in many cases, I would be doing the work myself. However, when estimating costs, I always put down what it would cost as if I hired it out. That way, in case I do have to hire out, I won't lose money. And if I, in fact, do it myself, I'm paying myself a reasonable salary for work performed.

Roof—$20,000

A proper wood roof in the original style would probably cost close to $20,000. The style was very labor intensive, and only a few roofers could do that kind of work.

Exterior Walls—$5,000

The house had clapboard on the outside, most of which appeared to be original. Replacing it wouldn't be difficult but would require peeling the old rotted boards away and replacing them with new boards. My estimate was $5,000.

Heating System—$7,000

Getting forced-air heat to all of the rooms (the only heat came from one old floor heater in the living room) would require cutting through floors and walls and would be prohibitively expensive. The less expensive way to go was individual electric wallboard heaters in each room. However, these are very costly to operate, and most buyers realize this. Installing them would cut back on the saleability of the home. I decided that forced air would be the way to go. The estimate was a minimum of $4,000, plus roughly $3,000 for rebuilding the walls and floors that had to be cut away.

Plumbing System—$9,000

The old plumbing system was shot. Drain pipes were corroded, broken, and leaking. The water pipes were old galvanized steel and corroded in countless places. The house would have to be replumbed with copper potable and plastic drain pipe. To replumb this two-story house, the cost would be about $9,000.

Electrical System—$7,000

The house had originally been outfitted for gas lighting. Sometime in the 1920s, the owner had added two-strand wiring, the kind where the thinly insulated wires are held about an inch apart by insulators placed every few feet. This is a building inspector's nightmare. The house would have to be rewired, with a new circuit breaker box installed. Because retrofitting meant cutting into walls, ceilings, and floors, the work would be more expensive than doing brand new construction. The estimate was $7,000.

Clean-up, Replastering, and Painting—$6,000

Based on what I had seen in the house, I estimated this work would cost $6,000.

Carrying Costs—$5,000

You have to pay the mortgage and utilities while you do the work. (Because taxes and insurance can be paid annually, you may want to not figure these in now but rather include them as part of your selling expenses.) If you live in the property, you can overlook this expense and call it your regular living costs. If not, add in a figure for this. I usually simply add in $5,000, which I hoped would cover at least three months, as an average figure. You may want to add more or less.

Transaction Costs

To the repair estimates, I added both the transaction costs of the purchase and resale. I knew from experience that the total transaction costs would total around 10 percent of the resale price.

$335,000 (Resale price) × 10% = $33,500 (Transaction costs)

I also calculated another 10 percent of the resale price, which I felt was the minimum profit I would expect for taking the risk of fixing up the house.

$335,000 (Resale price) × 10% = $33,500 (Minimum profit)

Arriving at the Purchase Price

Remember the basic formula:

Resale price – Total costs = Purchase price

I now subtract my total costs and expected profit from what I felt I could resell the house for and came up with my offering price.

$335,000 (Resale price) – $126,000 (Total costs)
= $209,000 (My offer)

Notice that to find the price you should pay, you work backward. You begin with the final sales price, then deduct your estimates of *all* expenses and costs, and what you arrive at, no matter how small it may be, is the correct price you should pay for the fixer.

———

FIGURE 5.1 *Estimate of Costs to fix Up Houses*

	$ 20,000
Exterior walls	5,000
Heating system	7,000
Plumbing system	9,000
Electrical system	7,000
Cleaning up, replastering, painting	6,000
Carrying Costs	$5,000
Profit	33,500
Transaction costs	33,500
Total	$126,000

Making the Offer

Much to my surprise, I found that Mrs. Smith's apparently low asking price of $285,000 was actually about $76,000 too high for me! If I paid what she wanted, I'd never be able to do the requisite work and make a profit. Indeed, I would lose a lot of money.

So I went to Mrs. Smith and showed her my figures. I pointed out that, regardless of who did the work, it would have to be done and would cost roughly what I estimated. She could, of course, save my 10 percent profit by doing the work herself, but I suggested that it might not be something she'd be willing or able to take on.

She countered by offering me cookies and milk. Then she asked me if I was trying to take advantage of an old lady. I assured her I was not, but at the same time I had no intention of letting an "old lady" take advantage of me.

We talked some more, and eventually she said she would come down another $5,000 or so in price but nothing like the amount I was offering. I thanked her for the cookies and milk, said that I simply couldn't pay more for the place, and left.

I kept track of Mrs. Smith's house and, about four months later, she sold it for about $270,000. Subsequently, I noticed that the new owners were fixing it up. I drove by occasionally, watching the work, until one day I noticed the place all boarded up. I made inquiries and found out that the new owners had not been able to keep up their mortgage payments and had abandoned the property. It was now in foreclosure.

I took a second look at the place. But the new owners had different ideas from mine. They had put on a cheap roof and started metal siding on the outside. They had made major cuts in the walls, floors, and ceiling inside, and the house was a mess. At that point, I saw no hope for it except as a scraper.

The Moral to the Victorian

I specifically chose the Victorian house for an important reason. While it's easy to pick out successful fixer stories, the most important lesson to be learned in the field is when to say no. It's better that you pass up five good deals than buy one bad one.

Nothing will sour you faster and more permanently than over-paying for a fixer. You will find yourself overwhelmed by costs, work, and a shrinking timeline. If you don't build enough "fat" into every purchase to allow for the necessary work, to pay yourself, and still make a profit, I guarantee you'll end up like the luckless buyers of Mrs. Smith's house.

Here's the one rule that you need to cut out of this book, paste over your desk, and look at before you make an offer on any fixer:

RULE

NEVER, NEVER, NEVER pay more for a fixer than what you can resell it for, less ALL of your costs plus your profit.

Remember, it's business. If you want to be a philanthropist, then do charitable work. But, if you want to make money, read that rule at least once a day, then follow it unswervingly.

What about Guesstimating Sheets?

One thing that allowed me quickly to get estimates of the value of the property and repair costs was the fact that I had a list of experts on whom I could rely. All I had to do was find a plumber, electrician, and roofer from my list of resources and give them a call. They returned estimates within 24 hours. That's not the way it works if you have to call people cold from the yellow pages. In Chapter 8, we'll discuss putting together your own "dream team" to help you become more successful in the fixer field.

It's very helpful to have a few guesstimating sheets, where you give your best estimate of cost, ready for any time you check out a property. That way, when you show up, you can make your calculations quickly and determine just how much you should pay.

Here are three sheets that I find indispensable (see Figures 5.2, 5.3, and 5.4). You will learn how to fill out and use these in Chapter 11, but a quick overview here will clarify the steps you need to follow.

FIGURE 5.2 *The Pricing Guesstimator*

Job	Cost Estimate	Time Required
Fix roof		
Fix outside walls		
Fix inside walls		
Paint outside walls		
Paint inside walls		
Landscape yard		
Fix heating system		
Fix air-conditioning		
Fix drain pipes		
Fix other plumbing		
Fix electrical system		
Install circuit box		
Fix bathroom(s)		
Fix kitchen		
Enlarge rooms		
Fix foundation		
Fix structure		
Other		

Use your own expertise to take as accurate a guess as possible at what any given job will cost you. In Figure 5.2, the Pricing Guesstimator, I've listed the most common work. You'll ignore some items and add others according to your particular fixer.

If your guesstimate from Figure 5.2 shows a possible profit, continue to Figure 5.3. This covers the same ground as Figure 5.2. However, here you're no longer relying on your figures but instead have at least a verbal estimate from an expert in the field.

FIGURE 5.3 *The Expert Advice Sheet*

Job	Cost Estimate	Time Required	Who'll Do It?
Fix roof			
Fix outside walls			
Fix inside walls			
Paint outside walls			
Paint inside walls			
Landscape yard			
Fix heating system			
Fix air-conditioning			
Fix drain pipes			
Fix other plumbing			
Fix electrical system			
Install circuit box			
Fix bathroom(s)			
Fix kitchen			
Enlarge rooms			
Fix foundation			
Fix structure			
Other			

To determine the maximum you should offer, you'll fill in the blanks in Figure 5.4 with the information from Figure 5.3, plus other information that you should already know.

Resale price – Total costs = Purchase price

FIGURE 5.4 *Calculating Your Maximum Price*

Probable Resale Price*	$
− Total cost of work to be done	
− Costs of purchase	
− Costs of resale	
− Carrying costs (unless you move in)	
− Unexpected "extras"	
− Your profit	
= Maximum amount to offer†	

*You got this information by checking out comparable house sales in the area (those that are already fixed up and are roughly the same in terms of location, size, number of bedrooms/bathrooms, quality of work, and so on.

† If you offer more, you won't make any money. Be careful of "coming close." When some would-be fixers get close, they go back and recalculate. This is usually a mistake. Your first calculations are based on cold facts. Your second calculations are often based on how much you can skim off the costs to make the deal. Invariably, your second calculations will be short. With a fixer, it's better that you estimate your costs too high than too low.

6 Accurately Calculating Costs

Before you buy a fixer you need to know—pretty darn accurately—how much it will cost to fix it up. Whether you're considering a house or another property, if you don't know your expenses, it's impossible to work back to figure out what you should pay. (See Chapter 5 for the formula for calculating the correct price.) And if you pay too much, you'll lose money when it comes time to sell. Even if you intend to live in the property for a period of time, you should make your calculations as if you were going to sell immediately so you don't build in a loss.

Knowing how much your expenses will be in advance, however, is only partly science. There's also a good measure of judgment, experience, and luck involved. As a result, your best guess is, in reality, only a "guesstimate"—a realistic estimate of what you calculate your true costs will be. In this chapter, we'll see how to make that guesstimate as accurate as possible.

Is It Really That Complicated?

I worked with a fellow some years ago who had a mind like a calculator. Philip would take into account all our costs and our as our profit or loss. He even played a game with our accountant who did the books at the end of the year. The day the accountant came in, Philip would write down on a piece of paper his guess at the profit for that year, seal it in an envelope, and hand it to the accountant. The accountant would then work for days on the books to come up with the profit figure. When the work was done, the envelope was opened. Philip was never more than $100 off!

Most of us, however, don't think like Philip. Indeed, I sometimes have trouble remembering a phone number I just heard, let alone the price of 17 gallons of paint or how much a drywall laborer will charge to replace three walls.

Keeping track of your funds is not just a matter of writing down figures; it also involves making projections. Many of the prices and costs you will need to handle will be for future work. It's fairly easy to keep track of expenses that you've already incurred. Worst case, you simply stick the invoices in a shoebox, and they're there later on when the accountant comes in. Estimates are a different ball game.

Estimates need not only to be written down but evaluated. You may get three or more estimates for a particular task. You may get separate estimates for labor and for materials. Different people will want to do the work differently. Hence, comparing estimates may be like comparing apples and oranges. Finally, there's the matter of whether you will hire someone to do the work or whether you'll do it yourself.

Trying to keep track of all this in your head, even for a small fix-up job like a kitchen or bath, will not only give you a headache but probably will result in costly errors. Therefore, no matter how big or small the job, no matter whether you'll just paint a few rooms or rebuild an entire house, I always urge you to use an estimating sheet.

Using Guesstimating Sheets

You were introduced to guesstimating sheets in Chapter 5. They will help you keep track of everything that needs to be done on a fixer and calculate the costs of repairs. You can easily create one yourself specifically for the job you have. You can obtain them from builders, who often have designed their own. They're also available in larger stationery stores, or you can use the one I've included at the end of this chapter (see Figure 6.1).

The point, however, is that you learn how to use such a sheet properly. If you do, it will save you a lot of time and money.

While our guesstimating sheet is fairly self-explanatory, and the basic method for using it is quite simple, the application is a bit trickier, and some areas deserve special attention, especially if fixers are new to you. Let's look at an example.

Jim and Mary are considering buying a fixer. Their goal is to get into a particular high-priced neighborhood and their only option because of limited funds and income, is a fixer. So they are looking at all the rundown houses they can find in that neighborhood.

For most people, the typical method of checking out a house is to wander through the rooms as an agent points out this or that. This method is fine for first scouting out a property. But once you identify a likely prospect as a fixer and before you make an offer, you need to go back and fill out a guesstimating sheet.

Jim and Mary identified two likely candidates. So they went back to each, accompanied by an agent in one case and an owner in the other. They explained to each that they were thinking of fixing up the property if they bought it. What they were doing now was taking an hour or two to get an estimate of what it would cost to do the work.

HINT

The minute you bring out your guesstimating sheet at a fixer, chances are the owner or the agent will tell you that they've already had a builder give an estimate and it's for X amount of money. Never mind what they say; do the estimating yourself. At this stage, someone else's estimate may be interesting, but you need to know what to the work will cost you, not them.

Jim and Mary carefully identified each problem with the property that required fix-up. Once the problems were identified, the couple used their guesstimating sheet to come up with a total fix-up cost.

Of course, in the majority of cases, they didn't know the true cost, so they put down their estimate of what work and materials would be required and put a question mark where the price should go, to be filled in later.

Bring a Camera

Jim and Mary also brought a camera along. Remember that, while needed work may seem perfectly clear when it's right in front of us, when we leave and then think about it, we may confuse one room with another, work needed on the bathroom sink with that needed on the kitchen sink, and so forth.

So Mary brought a camera along. No, she didn't photograph everything that needed to be done in the house. They knew that a complete painting inside and out was necessary, so photographing the walls was unnecessary. But she did take pictures of the shower stall in one bathroom and the tub in another, both of which would require fixing. Likewise, she took a picture of some holes in the outside wall and the chipped kitchen sink. She also kept a notebook page of where each picture was taken—which property and which room. These would prove helpful later, when she and Jim tried to get more specific cost estimates.

Finally, when they had noted everything they could and taken pictures of anything that they might forget (or that could be confusing upon reflection), they left the house. They repeated the process at the other house. Their next task was to nail down accurate prices. We'll cover that shortly, but first, let's consider whether their guesstimating sheet was all-inclusive.

How to Ensure You Are Including All Possible Fix-up Work

Every job is different. You may go into a house and discover that the hardwood floors need to be fixed. Some boards have dry rot. Others have termite damage. Parts of the floor need to be pried up and replaced. Some underneath supports may need work. Then there's sanding, priming, varnishing, and whatever else may be needed to finish that task.

Does your guesstimating sheet cover everything that needs to be done for flooring? You should have categories for:

- Removing damaged wood
- Replacing flooring
- Bracing supports
- Nailing and filling nail holes
- Sanding
- Priming and varnishing

If you're using a standard form, even the one presented at the end of this chapter, the appropriate categories won't always be there. As a result, you need to be able to add categories to fit the job.

HINT

Never make the job fit your guesstimating form. If you do, chances are some expenses will be left out or underestimated. Add categories on your guesstimating sheet as you go.

Your fixer also may require replastering walls, rehabilitating an old furnace, refurbishing stained glass windows, painting, and landscaping. Most of these general categories will be on your sheet, but you need to be able to add specifics and categories as needed.

Are Your Price Estimates Realistic?

The whole idea behind a guesstimating sheet is that you determine what a particular job will cost. However, as noted earlier, you really may have no idea what it will cost, particularly if you're new to the game. So what do you do?

What you need to do is research. You need to spend some time finding out what things cost. This may involve making calls to tradespeople to find out how much they charge for particular work, by the hour and by the job. It may mean making appointments with them to go and look at the property. And it certainly will mean getting up to speed on what materials cost.

Finding Out Hourly Costs

You may need a plumber, an electrician, a painter, a person to install drywall, another person to handle taping and texturing of drywall, and so on. You need to know how much these people charge to do the work. How do you find out?

Simple. You call them. In Chapter 8, we describe creating a dream team and networking with tradespeople. Both of these techniques will help you quickly find out about costs. However, when you're first starting out, you'll have to pick up the phone book and make some calls. For painting, plastering, installing drywall, carpeting, and floor refinishing, you must have fairly accurate measurements. For plumbing and wiring, the tradespeople will want to know when the house was built, if the systems were ever updated and when, how many rooms are in the house, and so on.

You can often get these answers right over the phone. While tradespeople always insist they need to see the job to give any sort of accurate estimate, I've never had them refuse to tell me what they would charge *in general* for the job, as long as I preface my question by: "All I want is a ballpark figure. I'm not going to hold you to it. I just want to know in general."

Getting Job Estimates

On the other hand, particularly if this is all new to you, you may not have any idea of what really needs to be done. Yes, the bathroom is a mess. The tub has deep scratches and gouges in it. There's a crack in the sink. One cabinet door is off. But must everything be replaced? What about the sink and tub fixtures? What about the plumbing behind them? In short, if you're new to the field, how do you know what needs to be done?

In this case, you need to get someone out to see the property who is qualified to do the work. Again, if you have a network or a dream team, getting an estimate is easy. If you don't, it's a bit trickier but certainly not impossible.

First, you must determine whom you want to talk with. If the project is a bathroom, a plumber certainly comes to mind. But other people do bathroom design; they work with plumbers but aren't plumbers themselves. Also, some people refinish tubs and sinks without replacing them.

How do you learn about these alternatives? The only way is to talk to people in the trade, as many and as often as possible. And when you have a specific problem, ask people to come out to give you hard estimates.

Once again, if you're new, you'll have to let your fingers walk through the phone book to find people. Also, try the local newspaper where those who are more aggressively seeking work may advertise. Don't overlook signs on shops in the area. And don't forget to check the Internet.

Keep in mind, however, that if you don't already have a relationship with someone from whom you want to get an estimate—particularly a pro like a plumber or electrician—you'll go on the bottom of their list. Chances are they're working during the day and will only be willing to come out at night, and then after they've already looked at the jobs who called in before you. Be prepared to wait, or make a contingent offer based on later inspections.

CAUTION

If you're going to get more than one estimate for the same job, try not to have those giving the estimate be at the job site at the same time. There's too much chance they'll compare notes, and you'll get very similar quotes. Logistics here can be tricky. You may need to schedule several people at different times over a couple of days. If the house is vacant, that shouldn't be a problem. However, if an owner or, even worse, a tenant, is there, scheduling could be quite challenging.

My advice here is to be demanding and persistent. Remember, you're in the driver's seat when it comes to making an offer. A seller who wants to sell will have to do what it takes to get you to make that offer. If it means letting you and your estimators in five times during the day, then that's what it takes. Besides, usually with a fixer, the seller is aware that the evaluation process is likely and is ready to accept it.

When tenants are involved, however, getting access to the property is more problematic. The tenants have their privacy to lose and nothing to gain by letting you in repeatedly. Again, be determined and persistent. If a problem arises, let the landlord/owner handle it. Worst case scenario, you may not be able to get in. But, if the property looks like a terrific deal, you may want to make a guesstimate without an expert's estimate. If you do, however, leave a little extra in your offer for error.

Reluctant Estimates

One last problem may occur in getting an estimate from someone in the field. One of the first questions they are likely to ask is, "Do you own the property?"

These people intensely dislike going out and making estimates on deals that never get done. It's a waste of their valuable time. Hence, what they are really asking is whether or not you're a player. Are you the person who can hire them?

An owner certainly is. A buyer with a deal in escrow certainly is. But someone who's thinking about making an offer that may or may not get accepted is doubtful. Of course, if you have a network and a dream team, getting your offer accepted may be no problem. If you don't, you may need to tie up the property via a contingent offer before you're able to get people out. Or you may just get lucky and find some really anxious tradespeople who want to bid on jobs and get to know people like you.

Pricing Materials

You may need to install a new door, window, shower enclosure, kitchen sink, fireplace insert, or almost anything else that you'll find in a house. You may need to know the cost of copper piping or a new circuit breaker box. How much are shingles that are approved for your area? Today, some locales require special fireproof composition shingles; no wood is allowed. Some home-owners' associations only approve certain types and brands of materials. Then there's the little stuff like nails, screws, and the tools themselves. What do all of these cost?

Assuming that you have a pretty good handle on what you want and need to do, your next stop may be a hardware store. In the past, hardware stores were the priciest of places to shop. If you weren't in the trade and able to buy wholesale, you often paid two or three times as much for hardware as those in the trade.

Today, however, with various discount home maintenance franchises springing up all over the country, it's possible to purchase materials at a reasonable cost, often for less than builders, as we'll see in a moment.

First, let's consider estimating materials costs. Most, but not all, materials that you'll need can be found at a discount hardware store. You may be able to get some things you need for less by shopping around, but a big discount hardware store often will give you a good average price. I suggest you simply go to one of the hardware behemoths and price everything you need. Within a few hours, you should have quite a detailed materials price list.

For unusual items, you'll need to shop around. For example, recently I needed to get the price on a septic sump pump. This is a special pump that goes into a septic tank and pumps liquid waste uphill to a leech field. You'll usually only find it in rural areas without municipal sewer systems.

None of the discount hardware stores I checked carried one. In fact, it wasn't carried in any city within 50 miles of the property. However, using the Internet, I did locate an out-of-state plumbing supply house that not only had sump pumps but over 35 different brands and models. They even put an engineer on the phone who, when I told him the height the pump would have to push the liquid and the size of the tank, gave me the precise size of pump I needed. And they were willing to ship it directly to me, if and when I ordered it using a credit card. As I said, you may need to shop around, but ultimately you will (at least in every case in which I've been involved) be able to get a material's price, often over the phone.

Finding a Single Source

A few paragraphs ago, I mentioned that it was possible for you not only to get good prices but also to get prices that were actually lower than what builders would pay. How can you do that? It works something like this.

Most people assume that when they need to buy something, virtually anything, they must pay top dollar because they need to buy only one. You need a sink, so you go to the hardware store and buy one for close to full retail price. Even in a discount hardware store you're paying more than you need to.

We all assume that there are economies associated with buying in quantity. We've actually been conditioned into believing this from the time we were children. You go to the store to buy a pair of stockings, and they are $5 apiece. But, if you buy three pair, you can get them for $12, or $4 apiece. The seller is willing to give you a discount because you buy in quantity. Sound familiar?

We all assume the same thing happens with building materials. We need to buy a shower enclosure. We go to a hardware store, even a discount hardware store, and buy one. We assume that whatever price we pay, it's got to be higher than a builder who goes directly to the manufacturer and buys 50 of these for a tract of houses, right?

The truth is far different, however. When we need to purchase only one of an item, we may actually be at an advantage. We may be able to get a better price than that builder who purchases 50. The reason? The builder's houses must all look alike, or a buyer may want one house with the sink from another and tub from a third. We, on the other hand, may be able to take advantage of closeouts, remainders, and special sales.

No, such opportunities are not predictable, and often you must act fairly quickly. But it does work. When you need to buy only one of an item, you can often get it for a fraction of its retail cost—if you look carefully.

All hardware stores, particularly the large discount ones, are try-ing to get rid of closeout items all the time. They often mark items 50 percent off or more. Yes, sometimes the fixtures have a defect, but often it's only a scratch that you can hide or remove. Yes, the strategy is hit-or-miss, and you can't predict what you'll find at any given time. But, if you're constantly on the lookout (as you will be, the more fixers you do), you'll buy generic items when they're available at closeout. And when you need something specific, you may check four or five stores before you find it at a price you want to pay.

Thus, when pricing materials, if you're the sort who's willing to nose around to find the closeout, the remainder, or the special sale, you may be able to take a percentage off the prices you see for the items sold at retail (even at discount) on store shelves. For myself, when it comes to big-ticket items such as sinks, doors, tubs, etc., I always figure a third less than the prices I see. Yes, estimating that way is a gamble. But I've had enough success that I just know that, before I actually need the item but after I've bought the property, I'll be able to find just one at a fraction of the cost I usually see posted.

Note that this also applies to labor. When a builder hires labor, the builder must deal with subcontractors, unions, and pay scales. On the other hand, when you hire labor for your one job, you may be able to deal with an individual worker, often one who is doing the job on personal time. As a result, you may be able to negotiate a better price.

When you're asking a professional plumber or an electrician to bid on a job as part of their regular work, you'll likely get a full-priced bid. However, if the tradesperson is doing the work on off hours to make a little extra money, they may be willing and able to do it for much less. After all, cutting prices benefits both of you, saving you money and giving the tradesperson some extra work. However, this approach usually only works when you have a small, single project to do. On the other hand, it's a great way to draw a professional in the trade into your dream team.

Be the Best Guesstimator

Figure 6.1 gives you an idea of how complex your estimate must be. Bad figures, or failing to include items, mean you'll lose the bid or you'll lose money on the fixer.

FIGURE 6.1 *Guesstimating Sheet*

Task	Hours	Labor		Materials	Overhead
		You	Hire It		
KITCHEN					
Cabinet, cleaning					
Cabinet, painting					
Cabinet, refinish					
Cabinet, repair					
Cabinet, replace					
Ceiling, paint					
Ceiling, repair					
Counter, clean					
Counter, Formica® install					

FIGURE 6.1 *Guesstimating Sheet (continued)*

Task	Hours	Labor		Materials	Overhead
		You	Hire It		
Counter, granite install					
Counter, tile install					
Counter, other install					
Counter, repair					
Counter, wood edge install					
Dishwasher, fix					
Dishwasher, replace					
Electrical, fix					
Electrical, replace					
Faucets, replace					
Faucets, replace washer					
Floor, cleaning					
Floor, linoleum install					
Floor, tile install					
Floor, wood install					
Garbage disposal, fix					
Garbage disposal, replace					
Plumbing, fix					
Sink, cleaning					
Sink, repair					
Sink, replace					
Smoke alarm, install					
Stove, fix					
Stove hood, fix					

FIGURE 6.1 *Guesstimating Sheet (continued)*

Task	Hours	Labor		Materials	Overhead
		You	Hire It		
Stove hood, replace					
Stove, replace					
Wall, paint					
Wall, repair					
Window, cleaning					
Window, repair					
Other					
Other					
Other					
BATHROOM					
Cabinet, cleaning					
Cabinet, painting					
Cabinet, refinish					
Cabinet, repair					
Cabinet, replace					
Ceiling, paint					
Ceiling, repair					
Counter, clean					
Counter, Formica® install					
Counter, granite install					
Counter, tile install					
Counter, other install					
Counter, repair					

FIGURE 6.1 *Guesstimating Sheet (continued)*

Task	Hours	Labor		Materials	Overhead
		You	Hire It		
Counter, wood edge install					
Electrical, fix					
Electrical, replace					
Faucets, replace					
Faucets, replace washers					
Floor, cleaning					
Floor, linoleum install					
Floor, tile install					
Floor, wood install					
Sink, cleaning					
Sink, repair					
Sink, replace					
Smoke alarm, install					
Toilet, cleaning					
Toilet, replace					
Towel holders, replace					
Tub/shower, clean					
Tub/shower, curtain					
Tub/shower, door					
Tub/shower, clean drain					
Tub/shower, fix drain					
Tub/shower, refinish					

FIGURE 6.1 *Guesstimating Sheet (continued)*

| Task | Hours | Labor | | Materials | Overhead |
		You	Hire It		
Tub/shower, replace					
Wall, paint					
Wall, repair					
Window, cleaning					
Window, repair					
Wood rot, fix					
Other					
Other					
Other					
BEDROOM					
Cabinet, cleaning					
Cabinet, painting					
Cabinet, refinish					
Cabinet, repair					
Cabinet, replace					
Carpet, clean					
Carpet, replace					
Ceiling, paint					
Ceiling, repair					
Closet door, repair					
Closet door, replace					
Closet, paint					
Counter, clean					
Counter, repair					

FIGURE 6.1 *Guesstimating Sheet (continued)*

Task	Hours	Labor		Materials	Overhead
		You	**Hire It**		
Electrical, fix					
Electrical, replace					
Floor, cleaning					
Floor, wood install					
Smoke alarm, install					
Wall, paint					
Window, cleaning					
Window, repair					
Other					
Other					
Other					
LIVING ROOM					
Carpet, clean					
Carpet, replace					
Ceiling, paint					
Ceiling, repair					
Closet door, repair					
Closet door, replace					
Closet, paint					
Electrical, fix					
Electrical, replace					
Fireplace, clean					
Fireplace, fix					
Fireplace, replace					

FIGURE 6.1 *Guesstimating Sheet (continued)*

Task	Hours	Labor		Materials	Overhead
		You	Hire It		
Floor, cleaning					
Floor, wood install					
Smoke alarm, install					
Stairway, fix					
Wall, paint					
Wall, repair					
Window, cleaning					
Window, repair					
Other					
Other					
Other					
DINING ROOM					
Carpet, clean					
Carpet, replace					
Ceiling, paint					
Ceiling, repair					
Closet door, repair					
Closet door, replace					
Closet, paint					
Electrical, fix					
Electrical, replace					
Fireplace, clean					
Fireplace, fix					
Fireplace, replace					

FIGURE 6.1 *Guesstimating Sheet (continued)*

Task	Hours	Labor		Materials	Overhead
		You	**Hire It**		
Floor, cleaning					
Floor, wood install					
Smoke alarm, install					
Stairway, fix					
Wall, paint					
Wall, repair					
Window, cleaning					
Window, repair					
Other					
Other					
Other					
FAMILY ROOM					
Carpet, clean					
Carpet, replace					
Ceiling, paint					
Ceiling, repair					
Closet door, repair					
Closet door, replace					
Closet, paint					
Electrical, fix					
Electrical, replace					
Fireplace, clean					
Fireplace, fix					
Fireplace, replace					

FIGURE 6.1 *Guesstimating Sheet (continued)*

Task	Hours	Labor		Materials	Overhead
		You	Hire It		
Floor, cleaning					
Floor, wood install					
Stairway, fix					
Wall, paint					
Wall, repair					
Window, cleaning					
Window, repair					
Other					
Other					
Other					
ENTRANCE/ HALLWAY					
Carpet, clean					
Carpet, replace					
Ceiling, paint					
Ceiling, repair					
Closet door, repair					
Closet door, replace					
Closet, paint					
Electrical, fix					
Electrical, replace					
Floor, cleaning					
Floor, wood install					
Stairway, fix					

FIGURE 6.1 *Guesstimating Sheet (continued)*

Task	Hours	Labor		Materials	Overhead
		You	**Hire It**		
Wall, paint					
Wall, repair					
Window, cleaning					
Window, repair					
Other					
Other					
Other					
ATTIC					
Electrical, fix					
Electrical, replace					
Fans, fix					
Fans, install					
Insulation, add extra					
Insulation, install new					
Plumbing, fix					
Plumbing, replace					
Other					
Other					
Other					
BASEMENT/ GARAGE					
Electrical, fix					
Electrical, replace					
Floor, fix cracks					

FIGURE 6.1 *Guesstimating Sheet (continued)*

Task	Hours	Labor		Materials	Overhead
		You	Hire It		
Floor, replace					
Furnace/air, fix					
Furnace/air, replace					
Lights, fix					
Lights, install					
Plumbing, fix					
Plumbing, replace					
Stairs, fix					
Stairs, replace					
Water heater, fix					
Water heater, replace					
Other					
Other					
Other					
EXTERIOR					
Chimney, install					
Chimney, repair					
Chimney, replace					
Drainage, fix					
Driveway, clean					
Driveway, fix					
Driveway, replace					
Entrance, clean					
Entrance, paint					

FIGURE 6.1 *Guesstimating Sheet (continued)*

Task	Hours	Labor		Materials	Overhead
		You	**Hire It**		
Fence, install					
Fence, paint					
Fence, repair					
Front door, clean					
Front door, install					
Front door, paint					
Gutters, clean					
Gutters, fix					
Gutters, install					
Lawn, plant					
Lawn, reseed					
Patio, fix					
Patio, install					
Pool, clean					
Pool, fix					
Roof, repair					
Roof, replace					
Screens, replace					
Shrubs, plant					
Shrubs, trim					
Spa, clean					
Spa, fix					
Walks, clean					
Walks, fix					

FIGURE 6.1 *Guesstimating Sheet*

Task	Hours	Labor		Materials	Overhead
		You	Hire It		
Walks, replace					
Walls, paint					
Walls, patch					
Windows, clean					
Windows, replace					
Other					
Other					
Other					

7 Three Critical Steps to Success

It may seem that getting your property at the right price is the trickiest part of doing a fixer. After price, everything else seems anticlimactic. The truth is, however, that price is only the first step. Other pitfalls can hurt you along the way to a successful deal. Certainly, the next item to watch out for is structuring the deal.

What exactly do I mean by "structuring the deal"? Let me illustrate with a story about an auction. It was an estate sale of a home that had partly burned down. The owner had died in the fire, and now the property was being sold.

In an estate sale, the executor or administrator will typically solicit bids for the property and accept the highest. However, a court usually has to put its stamp of approval on the sale. This is done at an open hearing where the judge typically will open the bidding to anyone else, providing the next bid is a step (usually 10 percent) higher than the already accepted bid. That's where the auction comes in.

Mine was the accepted bid. However, I was fairly certain that others would bid in open court, because the property was such an attractive fixer. It was a fairly new house in a great neighborhood, with extensive cosmetic fire damage. Very little of the basic structure itself was damaged, just the interior walls, ceilings, fixtures, and so on. I was right. At least half a dozen other bidders jumped in, and very quickly the bidding moved higher than I wanted to go. So, following my rule not to bid higher than my pencil calculates I can profit, I dropped out.

The winner was a young man who was ecstatic with his purchase. I felt he had bid too much, but that was his problem. What next ensued, however, bordered on the comic.

The successful bidder was required immediately to put up a cashier's check for 10 percent of the purchase price, with the balance to follow within two days. This fellow, however, wanted to use a personal check, which the court was not willing to accept. Further, he said he wanted to negotiate the balance so that he could pay interest-only over the next six months while he fixed up the property. Then, when he resold it, he would pay off the balance.

The judge looked at the executor for about half a second before declaring the sale invalid and asking for the bidding to restart. All the bidders had remained, so we did it again, this time with a young woman winning, again—in my opinion—bidding too high.

She, however, was prepared. She had the cashier's check, had already arranged financing (which we'll discuss in Chapter 9), and agreed to pay the balance of the purchase price the next day. She also told us that she had arranged for the work to be done and was quite sure it could be finished in no longer than five weeks. And she smugly indicated that she already had a buyer in mind for the resale!

I had to give her credit for her planning—she had structured the deal from beginning to end. She knew what she was doing and how to do it. But when I met her several years later, she confessed that she had, indeed, paid too much for the property. However, because she had a solid plan, she still ended up making at least a tiny profit. If she hadn't structured the deal properly, however, she would have lost a bundle.

RULE

If you structure a good plan, you usually won't go astray when working with a fixer.

The three elements that should be structured into any fixer are:

1. *Time.* Planning day by day how you will use it

2. *Cash.* Knowing where you'll get it from and exactly when you'll need it

3. *Safety.* Planning escape paths in case something goes wrong with the deal

---

Notice that we're not limiting the "deal" strictly to the purchase agreement. Rather, the deal is the entire fixing up process, from purchase to ultimate resale.

Whenever you purchase a fixer, starting with your very first one, you want to structure your deal. You want to plan ahead so that every step and hopefully every possibility—good or bad—is covered.

How You Control Time: The Logistics of Repair

The first element in structuring your fixer deal is working with time. Time often represents the biggest stumbling block for most people who get into the field. Think of it in military terms. To fight a war, a general must have the army in the right place at the right time, along with all the right supplies for the army to do its job. Further, since the enemy never rests, "the right place" changes every day. Making all these things happen is called logistics, the science and art of procuring, maintaining, and transporting military equipment and personnel.

Fixing up a property is like a military campaign. It starts when you buy the property and involves getting cash and financing in the right amounts and at the right times to secure the purchase and to pay for the repair work. It also involves getting work done in the right order so that one project doesn't bump into another and you don't end up having to redo tasks. For example, you don't want to paint before you finish plastering the walls.

A fixer is essentially a logistics job. You need to know what needs to be done, where, and—most important—when. But because repairing a fixer often takes months, sometimes half a year or longer, how do you organize all this? How do you keep track of the myriad different chores that need to be done without losing one or two in the shuffle? The fixer field is rife with stories of people who didn't do the right things at the right time and paid dearly for it.

For example, I can remember a friend who was working on a fixer in the autumn and got so involved in inside work that he forgot to get the roof repaired. He was caught by fall's first rain and had a lot of water damage. Another friend of mine concentrated on getting the inside of the property perfect and ready for resale, only to realize she had forgotten to plant a lawn and landscape the outside, something that can take several months (if you do it inexpensively by seed). To get a timely sale, she had to transplant large bushes and trees and have sod laid—an unnecessarily expensive undertaking.

Create a Working Timeline

My personal solution to a fixer's logistics challenge is to create a working timeline. I plot, in advance and day by day, everything that I anticipate I'll need to do. Further, as new needs develop, I put them on my timeline.

I use a 12-month calendar, many varieties of which are available from any good stationery store. My calendar shows 12 months at a glance and leaves enough room for writing information on every date.

On this timeline, I can indicate graphically everything that needs to be done, as far as I know at the moment. My suggestion is that you consider doing something similar. You may want a wall calendar like I use, or you may use one of the many computer programs that are available to create something similar. I like the paper variety because I can see it easily all at once. The computer version, however, allows you unlimited space for writing notes on any given day. Or you can combine the two by writing a task on the paper calendar, with a time estimate, and key it to the full specs kept on your computer.

As we go through this book, particularly when it comes to the actual work you'll need to do, you'll want to note your timeline very heavily. When will you work on the kitchen? The bath? When will you call in the roofers? And so on. But for this chapter, we're going to consider the timeline only in general terms of the deal's overall structure.

How to Plan the Overall Deal on the Timeline

Plot on your timeline such things as the following:

- The day you'll raise the seed money (cash) you'll need for the deal
- The day you'll prearrange for the financing (get preapproved for the mortgage)
- The day you'll make the offer (Note: The first three items take place *before* you buy the property.)
- The day the offer is accepted
- The day you need to have your mortgage funded
- The day you need to deposit the final money into escrow (and the amount)
- The day you'll take possession
- The day repair work will start
- The days that you'll need money to begin different repair tasks
- The days your mortgage payments are due
- The days property taxes and insurance payments are due
- The day you anticipate work will be completed (covered in Part Three of this book)
- When you'll put the house up for sale
- How long you anticipate a sale to take

These are basic items for your timeline. You will certainly add many more as you develop the timeline for each fixer you do.

With a realistic and complete timeline, you will avoid the biggest fixer pitfall of all—surprises. Of course, you can't anticipate everything. But you will have planned out the big things, particularly when you'll need cash for various parts of your project.

Cash

We're going to assume here that you're able to get financing (a mortgage) to handle both the purchase and the work on your fixer. (We'll cover how this is done in Chapter 9.) What we're concerned about here is *when* you'll need the money and in what proportions of cash to financing. Let's look at it from the cash perspective first.

Coming Up with Cash

Cash means real money (out of your own pocket or someone else's) to start a deal. It is the hardest money to come by. Naturally, you want to use as little of your own as possible. Your goal is to use financing and perhaps partners' and investors' money to make the project run. However, the reality is that you will probably have to use some of your own cash.

What Will You Need Cash For?

Along the timeline for a fixer deal, you will need cash

- to cover your expenses while you plan ahead;
- for any down payment on purchase;
- for any closing costs on purchase;
- to buy materials and hire labor for each task;
- for incidentals, such as building permits;
- for mortgage payments while you work on the project;
- for insurance and year-end taxes; and
- to live on while you work on the project.

You don't want to borrow the entire amount you will need at the beginning of the project, because then you will be paying interest on money before you're putting it to work. You do need the money to be available whenever you need to pay a fee or start a new task.

When you add up all of the amounts represented in the list above, you quickly will see that you need an enormous amount of cash, distributed at many different times, to complete a fixer deal. It can add up to tens or hundreds of thousands of dollars. Will you have the money available *when* you need it?

Cash before the Deal

I call this "seed money," and it's number one on the list of needed cash. This is money that you'll need to cover your own expenses while you look for property. When you call someone in and pay for them to do an inspection and then don't buy the property, you'll still need seed money to pay for the inspection. (If you do buy the property, a friendly inspector can be paid when the purchase is completed.) If you put together a dream team of associates to help you with your fixer (see Chapter 8), call a meeting, and order lunch, you'll need cash to pay for everyone. It may not be much, but it's *cash*.

Seed money is very important, and you need to come up with it *by yourself*. It would be an embarrassment as well as a serious weakening of your position in the eyes of team members if you tried to get someone else to pay for this. Sometimes, the amount you'll need may be fairly small, only a few hundred dollars. But you'll need to spend it even though you probably won't see any immediate promise of results.

HINT

"Seed money" in reality is faith money. You put it up on faith. You use it to bet on yourself.

A word of advice: Don't scrimp on the little stuff. If necessary, be flamboyant. It will come back to you a thousand times over, even if you can't see results at the moment.

In a sense, seed money is the most important cash you can spend. It establishes you as the leader in the eyes of others, and it helps you to appraise a property more clearly. Some people, however, scrimp here because they can't see the light at the end of the tunnel. They take a potential ally or associate out to breakfast, but don't want to buy them the best meal. How does that look to the other person? If you can't afford or don't want to spend even such a small amount of money, what does that say about your confidence in yourself? Or about your confidence in your ability to put together a good fixer deal?

Cash at Time of Purchase

You can only legally come up with cash from two sources: savings and borrowings. Therefore, to reduce the amount of cash you need to take from your savings, you must increase your borrowing. Your first need for cash will come with the down payment and closing costs.

While you most likely will get an institutional mortgage (from a savings and loan, bank, mortgage banker, or other institution) for the majority of the purchase price, these lenders won't normally loan 100 percent of the purchase price on a fixer. Rather, they'll only loan a percentage, typically 80 to 95 percent. (We'll have more to say about this in Chapter 9.)

So, for your down payment, you'll probably need to come up with as much as 20 percent of the purchase price in cash. If the property costs $100,000, you may need as much as $20,000 in cash, plus perhaps another $5,000 including closing costs, for a total of $25,000.

How Do You Put in Less of Your Own Money?

You can put in less cash by doing any of the following:

- *Get a higher institutional mortgage.* Borrow 90 to 95 percent of the property's value.
- *Get the seller to carry either the whole mortgage or a second mortgage.* If the seller carries a second mortgage for 10 or 15 percent of the purchase price, your cash requirement for the

down payment drops to only 10 or 5 percent (or in some cases down to 0).

- *Get the seller to pay for your closing costs.* No rule says that a seller can't pay your closing costs. If the seller agrees to this, you retain more of your cash. In our example, you would save an additional $5,000 or more. The seller may agree to increase the price slightly and finance your closing costs. (See Chapter 9 for details on how and why this might be done.)
- *Arrange for the cash you need from relatives or friends.* You may be able to get others to put up part or even all of the money at the time of purchase in exchange for a promise to repay or even a percentage of the profits later on. Be aware, however, that institutional lenders often will not give a mortgage if the down payment is borrowed. (Certain Fannie Mae and other programs work around this. See Chapter 9 for solutions to this problem.)
- *Form a partnership.* In the previous chapter, we talked about putting together a dream team. You may be able to rely on your team for part or all of the initial money that you need.

How to Arrange for Cash During Fix-up

In addition to the cash you'll need when you purchase the property, you'll also need cash during the weeks and months you are fixing it up. Hopefully, you'll be able to accurately predict just when this money is needed. Now the question is, where do you get it?

You can get cash during the fix-up from any of these sources:

- *Your savings.* Many people who do fixers prefer to pay for all of the labor, materials, mortgage payments, and other costs out of their own funds. They reason that this way they aren't beholden to anyone, they don't have to agree to anyone else's terms, they don't have to pay interest on the money if it's borrowed, and they don't have to worry about the money being available just when needed. I prefer to do fix-up work this way myself, when possible. After all, I know that I'll get it all back, and more, on sale.

- *Borrow the money.* You may be able to borrow what you need from the seller. Or you may arrange for a construction or home equity loan from an institutional lender. You may even borrow it on credit cards, if you have a solid plan for repayment.
- *Get it in trade.* If you have a dream team, you may arrange to have much of the labor and even materials traded out for a share of the profits. But be careful if you do this. Everyone always seems to want a bigger share of profits than their share of work warrants. Getting concise estimates for the work may solve such disputes.
- *Take in partners.* Your dream team members may be willing to contribute, as may friends and family. Again, however, this means you'll end up with a smaller share of the pie on sale.

Should You Make Your Cash Arrangements in Advance?

No matter how you arrange for your cash needs, what's vitally important is that the money be available at the right time. It won't do you any good to get money for a mortgage payment or to pay a roofer three months after you need it.

Remember that you aren't the only one who knows this. Lenders, whether institutional or private, know it as well. If they discover that you didn't plan ahead, they'll conclude that you don't really know what you're doing, that your other plans (including repayment) may be flawed, and that you may not be a good risk.

Let's look at an example of what *not* to do.

Janine bought a small, three-bedroom, one-bath home in a nice area of town. Cosmetically it looked okay, but it was a broken-back fixer because it had only one bathroom. The same home with two baths sold in the same area for around $70,000 more. Janine figured she would put in another bath for around $35,000 and then resell for a profit.

Unfortunately, she used up so much of her own funds making the purchase, halfway through the fix-up, she ran out of cash. She immediately tried to get a loan. By then, however, the house was hacked apart. No lender wants to make a loan when there is evidence of prior construction, because its mortgage could be jeopardized by a mechanic's lien. A mechanic's lien is a demand for payment for materials or services on a real estate project and can be filed by any unpaid supplier. Payment of the lien generally takes precedence over mortgages filed after the work started or the materials were delivered.

Lenders also didn't want to make any personal loans, because they were suspicious of her ability to repay now that she didn't have any more cash of her own and was fully committed, financially speaking, to the existing mortgage. Her friends and family felt the same way, even if they were more sympathetic. They said they just didn't have any money they could lend her.

Within a few weeks, Janine was in serious danger of losing her property because she couldn't make the mortgage payment. She considered giving up work on the house (which she was doing full-time) and getting a regular job at least part-time. However, getting cash flow started would take several weeks, and during this time, her repair work would slow or stop, payments due would mount, and she'd be even further behind.

Janine's problem was caused not so much by lack of cash as it was by lack of planning. If she had structured the deal so that from the onset, she had overestimated rather than underestimated the required cash flow, things would have worked out. If she had arranged for an additional loan at the beginning, she wouldn't have had trouble at the end.

RULE

Always remember that institutions, friends, and associates are usually willing to lend you money when you don't need it. It's when you're desperate that they won't let you have it!

Janine's story does, however, have a happy ending. Janine had two credit cards and was able to arrange quickly for two more. By taking cash withdrawals, she was able to cover her expenses and save the deal. However, she had to pay hefty interest charges, more than 20 percent, which ate into her profits.

I share this story to suggest that you'll do far better when fixing up if you use your timeline to plan when you'll need money and then arrange for it far in advance of the need. Janine had a good credit rating. If she had arranged for the new credit before any payments were late, she could have obtained much better rates.

Thus far we've been concerned with the elements of timing and cash. The third element to structure a deal successfully is safety. If you haven't built escape paths into your plan so you can terminate a deal without losing money, you endanger not only the current project but your ability to get into future fixers.

Safety: Structuring Escape Paths

The need for safety begins with the sales agreement, as opposed to the overall deal (which includes the purchase, all the fixing up, and the later reselling). In the sales agreement, you have the opportunity to put in contingency or "subject to" clauses. These are statements that say something like, "This purchase is subject to the buyer obtaining financing . . ." and then giving the terms of the financing you're looking for.

As a buyer of fixers, you always want to leave as many escape hatches for yourself as possible. Always include contingency clauses that allow you to back out of a deal without having the seller sue you or keep your deposit.

Why do you want these? There are many reasons, but the two best are that with a fixer, it seems that you are continually finding new work that needs to be done as the purchase progresses, and arranging additional financing tends to be tricky. Let's consider some problems that tend to crop up.

Remember that a typical purchase usually takes a month or longer to complete. During that time, you may inspect the property several times, and each time you do, another problem pops up. What do you do, for example, if the deal is ready to close and you discover a big crack in the heat transfer box of the furnace or a leak in the roof? With a standard transaction, the buyer typically gets only one shot at an inspection, and if problems become apparent later, too bad for the buyer. With a fixer, however, make sure you have the right to go back many times, to measure, to check things out in greater detail, and so on.

Include a contingency clause written into the sales agreement that states that the purchase is subject to there being no additional undiscovered or undisclosed problems before the close of escrow (when the title transfers to you). If problems are found, the clause states that the deal is open to renegotiation or cancellation.

Financing Contingencies

The same holds true with financing. In a regular purchase, the financing is usually straightforward. The buyer is obtaining a mortgage for a set amount of money. However, in a fixer deal, often the buyer is not only obtaining a mortgage for the purchase but may also be obtaining a construction loan (either separately or blended with the purchase mortgage) to do the repair work. While the purchase mortgage may come through fairly quickly, it may not be until the last day before the construction loan is approved. And you don't want the property unless you also can get a construction loan.

Therefore, a contingency clause that makes the purchase subject to obtaining financing for both purchase *and* fix-up construction, protects your project and your cash.

Other Contingency Clauses

You may want other contingency clauses structured into the sales agreement depending on the type of property you're buying. For example, your purchase may be contingent on an adjoining piece of property being zoned commercial or being rezoned residential. Your agreement could be contingent on how tenants leave the property after they move out. In short, there's no limit to the number of different kinds of contingencies you may want.

CAUTION

Every time you structure a contingency clause into the sales agreement, it protects you and gives you a better deal, but it weakens the seller's position. Add too many clauses, and the seller won't accept. Sometimes, to get your price, you may be forced to pass up some or all of your contingency clauses.

Also, unless you're experienced and knowledgeable in real estate, don't attempt to write the contingency clauses yourself. Have a competent attorney or real estate agent do it. You might have the best of intentions, but you could find you've created an unfulfillable condition or forgotten to include a method for removing a clause.

Do You Have a Rental Option?

Another safety valve that I try to structure into fixer deals has nothing to do with contingency clauses. Rather, it addresses how the fix-up work is planned.

What if, despite the best of planning, your funds for fixing up don't arrive as anticipated? Or what if you get sick during the fixing-up stage and can't complete the work you had intended to do yourself? Or what if the market for the property suddenly deteriorates and it becomes clear you won't be able to resell for what you had anticipated?

One option I like to keep open is the possibility of renting out the property. Any property that is habitable can be rented. The word *habitable* is the key. If you've knocked out the kitchen or the toilets or if it has an uncovered roof, it's just not habitable. The rest of the time, however, it may be. Often, the place can be made rentable with only a few days' modifying work.

I always try to structure the repairs so that the property is uninhabitable for the minimum amount of time. Whether I'm planning to live in the house or rent it out, I want to be able to switch horses in midstream, so to speak. I want to be able to stop fixing up the property and working toward a sale and instead make it habitable.

A few years ago, I bought a house that was in terrible shape. Cosmetically, it needed repainting, recarpeting, and a thorough cleaning. Structurally, it needed to be replumbed and rewired.

I anticipated that it would be vacant for three to five months while all this work was done. However, no sooner had I completed the purchase than a maintenance man at a nearby church approached me with a proposal. He said he and his family would be willing to move in at three-fourths of the normal rent. He wanted the place for a year.

During his time in the house, he would do many of the required tasks. He offered to do the painting and all of the cleaning. He'd agree to be gone for the few days when the water had to be shut off. The rest of the time the plumbing work could be done in stages with only part of the house unusable. He'd do the same for the electrical work.

In short, I could collect rent from the moment I bought the house, plus get some of the labor thrown into the bargain. The house wouldn't be vacant until it was ready to sell.

After I got glowing references from his current and previous employer, how long do you think I considered his offer?

He moved in immediately after the sale closed. During the course of the year, the house was fixed up and all of its problems cured. Eventually he did move out and I did sell. Looking back, I realize that we helped each other. He got a place to live at a reduced rent. I got rental income and quality labor.

RULE

Never overlook the rental option. Sometimes it can save you money. Sometimes it can save the deal.

Is the Land Value There?

Yet another safety valve, particularly when you're dealing with a severely distressed fixer, is to pay particular attention to the land's value. This is especially the case where there are structural problems. Here's an example where not paying close attention trapped a buyer in a deal.

My friend Shelley recently bought a home in a very nice section of Los Angeles. While most of Los Angeles is fairly flat, some homes, particularly in the more desirable areas, are built on the sides of hills. Unfortunately, the area is subject to flooding and earthquakes, meaning that those hills have an occasional tendency to move down onto the flatland.

The home Shelley bought was on a hill with loose soil. It had been damaged by an earthquake. The earth had moved and split the house in half. While each half was basically intact, the house as a whole had been condemned and written off by both the insurance company and the owner as a total loss. Needless to say, Shelley was able to buy it for a song, with the seller financing the sale and Shelley only putting 10 percent down.

After she spent ample time patting herself on the back for her bargain purchase, she set about fixing up the house. After many hours arguing with the building department, she got them to agree to a set of plans that called for several concrete trusses to be built under the remains of the existing two halves. Then, using her own money, she had the trusses built and placed and carefully had the two halves levered back into place and put together. It was an altogether creative solution to an apparently unsolvable problem. After some cosmetic work, the house looked great. You'd never know it had been a disaster.

Then she put it up for sale.

Her problems began when her potential buyers tried to get financing. Lenders all seemed aware of the problems that had occurred with the house and knew that it was still on unstable soil. The regular institutional lenders (like banks and savings and loans) wouldn't make a loan. When the only financing the buyers could get was from high-risk lenders who wanted a higher-than-market interest rate plus extra points, they were alerted to the seriousness of the problem and were scared off.

Shelley was eventually able to find buyers who were willing to accept the house's problems and the higher-than-usual financing, for a significant reduction in price. However, now Shelley found that it was impossible to obtain even minimal homeowners' fire and earthquake insurance on the property, and even the high-risk lender wouldn't lend without those. And so the second sale fell through.

Eventually, Shelley was forced to rent out the property. She had used a substantial amount of her own funds for the down payment and the repairs and was now unable to get the money out. She was stuck.

The moral here is that Shelley didn't look at the underlying value of the land. She only looked at the improvements, the house, and the problem. Yes, she found a solution for those. But the underlying value (or lack of value) of the land hadn't changed. It was a valueless or extremely low-value property. She had been trapped because her plan wasn't complete.

Whenever you are considering buying a fixer, one of the safety valves you should check is the land itself. The way to check is to ask yourself, "If things go terribly wrong, can I always sell the land, hopefully for most of what I have put into the property?" If the answer is no, look elsewhere.

You need the safety valve of land that is saleable. Be particularly careful when you buy property that is

- on hillsides,
- in flood plains,
- adjoining factories or large commercial developments,
- near dump sites,
- or
- near or on property formerly used for a gas station or landfill.

You must be able to resell the land alone for enough to cover your investment and expenses. You don't want to learn that a lender or insurer or government agency will block the sale.

Buy It!

8 Put Together Your "Dream Team"

Napoleon Hill, in his book *Think and Grow Rich,* stated the importance of a "mastermind" team. Put together a group of people with goals similar to yours, although they may come from different fields, with whom you can share and build ideas. They will give you support, plus open your mind to new directions you haven't considered yourself.

Hill's book became world famous as a model for self-motivation. Although his idea for putting together a mastermind team was intended for self-motivation, we can apply the basic concept to fixing up property. We'll call our group the "dream team." You put together a dream team of associates who will help you find, fix up, and resell properties at a much higher level than you could possibly do all by yourself. This team will work with you on projects and help you to be more successful, faster. First, however, consider why you need help at all.

Do You Have an "I'll Do It Myself" Problem?

A lot of people who would be successful at fixing up homes suffer from what I call the "Renaissance Man Perspective." They feel they can do everything themselves. Just as the ultimate Renaissance man, Leonardo DaVinci, was a great painter, scientist, engineer, and doctor, some people feel they can be a great agent, designer, financier, carpenter, and so on. Whatever the task, they believe they can do it well, probably better than anyone else.

If you believe that, then you'll spend a lot of time without receiving much in the way of rewards. Probably the greatest asset that you as a person who fixes up property can have is to know your limitations. If you've never plastered before, don't attempt to fix a plaster wall yourself—get a pro to do it. If you haven't arranged financing before, get help from a mortgage broker.

CAUTION

Two false presumptions:

1. You can always do a good job by yourself.

2. Doing it yourself always saves money.

Are You a "Too Determined" Do-It-Yourselfer?

At this point, I can hear many readers saying, "Hiring out defeats the whole purpose of getting a fixer. The whole point is to saave money by doing it myself."

Let's consider an example that I ran into not long ago.

A good friend, Peter, bought a broken-back property. It only had one bathroom in an area where anyone who buys a home for top dollar expects at least two bathrooms.

Peter's plan was to convert a closet off a second-floor master bedroom into a second bath. He did the design himself; secured the plans; ripped out the closet; hauled the tub/shower, toilet, and sink upstairs; installed them; plastered the walls; and did everything else on his own.

Along the way, he had many delays. Because the upstairs drain wouldn't line up with the first-floor drains, he had to take out part of a ceiling and wall below. The building department repeatedly refused to accept his plumbing work. He had to keep doing it over and over until, finally, the inspector took pity and showed Peter how to do it so it would pass inspection.

Then Peter couldn't get the tub/shower into the former closet because the doorway was too small. So he had to rip out a section of that wall. Unfortunately, it was a bearing wall and that caused the roof to sag. He not only had to repair the wall but the roof as well. When he attached the toilet, he didn't seat it properly. It required a correctly placed wax seal, and the first time he flushed it, water gushed out all over the floor, soaking the new carpet he had put in!

Now I'm sure some people would credit Peter with his spunk and put all his difficulties down to a learning experience. However, I talked with Peter afterward, and he said he had hated every minute of it. It was a frustrating experience, and the only thing he said he really learned from it was to stay away from fixers. Getting the bathroom done had taken him nearly three months. It cost him a small fortune. And the final result did not look good. It looked like the bathroom had been slapped together by an amateur, which was the truth. His work lacked the professional appearance buyers like to see, so he had trouble reselling the property.

The moral of Peter's story is that doing a fixer by yourself, unless you are an expert in many areas, is often more costly, is more time consuming, and has poorer results than if you hire the work out. Further, it can discourage you from working on fixers. While it's important to tackle jobs that may be a little bit harder than you're used to, it's equally important not to be overwhelmed by tasks that are nearly hopeless for you.

Now, I'm not suggesting that Peter should simply have called in a builder and said, "Put a bathroom there." That undoubtedly would have been even more costly. But, at critical stages along the way, he should have gotten workers who knew what they were doing to tackle the job. What were those stages?

1. Design (including the kind of fixtures that would fit)
2. Rough plumbing and electrical (including advice on how to install fixtures yourself)
3. Plastering, carpeting, finishing—as needed

If Peter had called in experts just when he needed them, doing all the other work of which he was capable, the job wouldn't have cost that much. And the job would have been done faster and better. Instead of its being a frustrating experience for him, it would have been a good learning event that would have enabled him to do even more himself the next time.

RULE

Don't be penny wise and pound foolish when it comes to fixing up.

Do what you can.

Know what you can't do, and call in the experts.

How Do You Build Your Own Dream Team?

Thus far, we've talked about hiring experts to help you in areas where you're deficient. While this is always a good thing to do, now we're going to put a different perspective on it. Instead of "hiring," we're going to consider "partnering."

Let's suppose that the first Monday of every month at 8:00 AM, you met with a group of "partners" who all were interested in buying properties, fixing them up, and selling them for a profit. The group would be informal, held together by common interest. The only time you would legally become partners is if and when you ventured together to buy a property. Then an attorney would draw up the appropriate documents making whomever in the group who wanted to participate formal partners or participants in a limited liability corporation. However, that's down the road.

Who should be in this group? There might be a number of tradespeople, such as a plumber, an electrician, and a roofer. Additionally, there might also be an architect, a real estate agent, a mortgage broker, and an accountant. And then there would be you, a full- or part-time entrepreneur devoted to successfully fixing up properties.

Consider what you all might discuss each week. The agent might say that she's seen two properties come back onto the market in the last week, either of which might be excellent choices as fixers. They are in good areas and in various stages of disrepair—one a scraper and the other a rejuvenator. The owners had tried unsuccessfully to sell them for nearly half a year, had taken them off the market, and were now putting them back on at realistic prices.

Then the plumber chimes in that he has seen another property that might make an excellent fixer. He had recently fixed a leaking water heater there. Now, however, the owners had died, and the property was in the hands of an executor who wanted to get rid of it because it was too old and had too many problems to rent out or sell at a good price.

Then the accountant chimes in that he has a client who owns a rental she wants to dump. The last tenants hadn't paid their rent for months, and before leaving they trashed the place. It needs cleaning, new carpeting, and some new fixtures—a true cosmetic fixer. The owner is willing to accept a very low price if she could sell quickly.

Instantly, you have four potential fixers to consider. You're the deal maker, so you agree to check out each one.

You spend the next two days looking at each of them. When you call on the roofer of the group in two cases for his expert help, he's there instantly, giving you the answers you need. You already have advice from the plumber on one property.

Eventually you narrow the field to two of the houses. Now you call on the architect for ideas on what would be best to do. Then the mortgage broker quickly comes out. You tell her you've selected one property over the others, and she tells you what kind of financing you could get and the best rates.

Next you call on the agent, who gets all the comparables so you can easily see what the property should sell for, once it's fixed up. Then you check with the accountant on the tax angles. Last, you go to see the seller and his agent to get a feeling for how amenable he would be to your offer. The seller seems anxious to accept a reasonable price.

After a week, you're ready. You meet again with the group and present your proposal. You describe the property, its current condition, what you would do to it, and its potential. Group members who have seen the property back you up. When you're finished, you ask who would like to participate.

The architect says he'll put in cash because he expects a good return on his money. The tradespeople offer their work in exchange for a chunk of the profit when the property sells. The agent will accept a lower commission in exchange for the resale listing. The mortgage broker can shave a bit off the financing costs in exchange for financing through her. And so it goes.

By the time you're finished, you have a deal made in heaven. You have all the support you could possibly want. You have the tools to buy the property, get the repairs done right, and sell it quickly. Further, *you* don't need to put in all the cash, all the work, or all the effort.

Of course, in exchange for this, you don't get all the profit. But would you have gotten such a sweet deal without your dream team?

The whole point here is that each person brings something to the table. No one member really has the time, expertise, money, or enthusiasm to do it all. But, by combining the skills of the group, you create the framework around which such a project can succeed. Further, along the way, you end up doing lots and lots of fixers and everyone does very well.

Do You Have the Keys to Form a Dream Team?

If I've sold you on the concept of a dream team, the next step is figuring out how to put one together. This usually requires one key person—a deal maker (you)—who has the fire and determination to make it all work. You should always remember that around you are many, many people who are willing to participate but who simply don't know how to get the ball rolling or are unsure of how to make things happen. Further, the participants on the dream team are not there to do anybody but themselves a favor. One way or another, they stand to benefit by the actions of the team. The agent will get a commission (or part of one) that she would not otherwise get. The tradespeople get work that they otherwise would not get.

Everyone on the team will be paid for their contribution in one form or another.

The whole purpose of the team, in fact, is to generate business. You get help in areas in which you are deficient and learn some new skills. You also get access to properties you might otherwise miss.

Where do you find the participants? As you meet tradespeople and work with them, if you find they are honest and eager to do more, you may suggest a weekly meeting with them. You don't need to lay the whole concept out immediately. You can just say you'd like to meet with them on a regular basis to discuss opportunities. You can do the same with your accountant, agent, and others.

Expect a wide variety of reactions. Some people will be wildly enthusiastic—especially agents! Others may not even consider the idea and won't show up. But if you're persistent and make the regular meeting a ritual (you're there even if only one or two other people show up), eventually people will climb on board.

Also, each person you talk to knows others. Initially, invite as many as possible to attend. You want to be inclusive, not exclusive. You have plenty of time to be exclusive once your team is up and working.

Don't overlook your social contacts. You may meet someone who's an accountant or a bricklayer at your church or temple, at your kid's preschool or soccer game, or through a friend at your club. Talk with them. Talk up the idea of a dream team, particularly if you've already set up a regular meeting time and place.

What really brings the team together is a success, and it only takes one. Find a property, use the team's resources, fix it up, and sell so that everyone makes a profit. A success will encourage the team to stick together for many years to come.

Where Do You Find Expert Help?

You can always rely on the phone book. I've done that on occasion when I had no other alternative. However, the phone book usually shows dozens of names. How will you tell who does really good work without charging an arm and a leg for it?

My suggestion is that you go with recommendations. Finding good experts to help you is sort of like solving a jigsaw puzzle. As soon as you find one piece that fits, it suggests where others should go. As soon as you find one good person, they will suggest others who will help you.

Here are some sources you can tap when you're first looking.

Agents. Many real estate agents work on fixers on the side. They buy properties, clean and rebuild them, and offer them for sale. We'll have more to say about this shortly, when we discuss the fine points of building your own dream team. For now, however, remember that these agents often can recommend workers in many fields, such as plumbing, electrical, plastering, carpentry, painting, and so on. Typically these recommendations are based on having worked directly with these people.

Friends in real estate. The agent from whom you buy a property or who is showing you a property is usually a good source. So are the insurance agent, the attorney you use, and other people involved in deals. If your contact doesn't know anything about fixing up, ask if someone else in the office does. Because you may work with several agents when you're looking for the right property, along the way you should run into several good sources. They are usually more than willing to help you out, in the hopes of getting a listing when you offer the property for resale.

Building inspectors. Visit your local city or county hall and talk to one of the field inspectors. Chances are that, if you're doing any kind of renovation work, you'll need a permit and will have to deal with these people anyway. While inspectors often are very busy, I've found that if I come in late in the afternoon after they've returned from their inspections, they often don't mind chatting over a cup of coffee. Describe the kind of work you'll be doing and ask them who in the area does good work at a reasonable price. These field inspectors may be able to give you some excellent leads.

Friends, relatives, and associates. Chances are, someone you know has had some sort of work done in the not-so-distant past. Ask for a recommendation. Did the person do a good job? Did they charge a lot or a little? Would the person you know use that tradesperson again? But be careful with personal recommendations. Gauge who's doing the recommending. Sometimes others use far different standards from yours. Your friend Joanne may rave over someone who built custom cabinets for her. However, Joanne may be very well-off and used to paying top dollar for an expert to do a job from start to finish. You, on the other hand, may be looking for someone who's willing to do only part of the job (you'll be doing the rest) and charge cut-rate prices. In exactly this situation, when I was looking for a carpenter to help me fix up a kitchen, I called the custom cabinetmaker and then went over and talked to him. It quickly became obvious to both of us that I wasn't looking for the kind of work he performed. But he was able to direct me to a carpenter/handyperson who was just perfect for the job.

Advertisements. If none of the above works for you, you will probably have to resort to looking at ads. I consider this method the weakest because you really don't know whom you're getting without a personal recommendation. Check out local newspaper ads. Search bulletin boards at supermarkets, pharmacies, and hardware stores; often tradespeople post small ads there. Search the Internet for the people and skills you need.

Locator services. Less helpful, from my own experience, have been services that offer to recommend local people to you for no fee. You telephone, tell them what kind of person you want, and they give you a name and a number. The problem here is that these services often are supported financially by the people who are being recommended. A worker who wants to be recommended pays a fee to be listed. Some services do basic screening to check credentials, but not always.

Should You Check Them Out?

No matter where you get recommendations, be sure that *you* check out the tradesperson. I always ask for the names and phone numbers of at least three people who have used them before. Anyone who's been in the business for even six months should be able to provide you with three references.

Then I call each reference and try to determine not only what kind of work was done but the relationship of the worker to the recommender. For example, if I'm talking to a plumber's brother-in-law, I'm less likely to put faith in the recommendation than if I'm talking to someone unrelated to the plumber!

When you make these calls, you often will rely on the words of total strangers. But it's better than not making the calls at all.

What "Vehicle" Should the Dream Team Use?

One of the problems with working with partners, even dream team partners, is how to formalize the relationship. It's okay to say, "When we finish, you'll get paid out of the profits," and shake hands on it. However, a lot of water can flow under the bridge between the handshake and the time the property sells and money gets distributed. It's better for all concerned to have a formal, written agreement so that they know exactly where they stand. This is an excellent reason for having an accountant and an attorney as part of your team—they can suggest the best format and wording for your agreement.

You may want a formal partnership agreement that's used on every deal you do. Or a contract specifying the work to be performed and the distribution of profits separately for each deal may work best. Decide what your team wants and what's best for all of you.

I formed my first dream team more than 30 years ago, and although we have long since gone our separate ways, I still occasionally bump into one of them and we reminisce about the deals we did—great and small.

Try putting together your own fixer's dream team. You will reap rich rewards if you do.

Guide to Finding Expert Help and Building a Dream Team

- Check with real estate agents for recommendations.
- Call your local building inspector for referrals.
- Check with friends, relatives, and associates for recommendations.
- Check out advertisements in the papers, on bulletin boards, and on the Internet.
- Call all references.
- Begin having dream team meetings on a regular basis and invite tradespeople with whom you've worked.
- Talk up your dream team idea at social gatherings, at work, and wherever you find a receptive audience. Ask people to attend your meetings.
- Strive to diversify. You don't need seven agents and one carpenter. Once you've got someone who fills a particular need, look for people in other areas.
- Get going on a project. Nothing brings the team to life like a hands-on fixer.
- Keep records of whom to keep on the team and whom to drop.
- Persist! Rome wasn't built in a day. Bill Gates didn't make his fortune overnight. Your dream team won't get off the ground at the first meeting. But keep at it and infuse others with your determination. You *will* get results!

9 Get Your Financing Ducks in a Row

Finding a great fixer is only half the battle. Getting the cash to buy it and do the fix-up work is the other half.

Very few people in the field work on a strictly cash basis, for obvious reasons. Nearly everyone borrows to make their deals, and chances are, you're no exception. You'll need to arrange financing to make it all work.

Fixers, however, can present special problems when it comes to finding money. Some lenders simply won't touch them. Other lenders will only give reduced mortgage amounts at higher interest rates and with more points. Finally, many lenders will want their borrowers to have better than average credit, which for many entrepreneurs can be the toughest obstacle of all. In this chapter, we'll deal with these and related problems and see how to overcome them.

HINT

Pay special attention *early on* to financing your deal. Get enough funds to do the whole deal from start to finish. And don't get buried by an overwhelming interest rate or too-high lending costs for your financing.

Can I Finance 100 Percent of the Deal?

The availability of 100 percent financing is probably the number one question most prospective borrowers have. The answer is yes, but strings are attached.

Real estate financing in general (as with most financing) is set up on the basis of risk and reward. Naturally, the lenders want to minimize their risk and at the same time maximize their reward. Over the years, they have discovered that the best way to do this is to make real estate loans only to individuals who are committed to the property on which the mortgage is offered. The greater the commitment, the better the loan.

How do you show your commitment to a property? By putting your own money into it and by moving in yourself. Lenders feel that, if the borrowers have some of their own money invested and are actually living there, if something goes wrong, they are much more likely to fight to save that property. In the face of a market downturn, a lost job, even illness, they'll fight to make the mortgage payment (the lender's reward) and avoid foreclosure (the lender's risk).

HINT

Lenders are in the business of loaning money, not owning property. The very last thing they want is to take back a property through foreclosure. That's why they try to be as careful as possible when making the loan, to be sure the borrower can and will repay.

How much money do lenders feel the borrower should put into the property? Technically, the amount should be enough to cover any lender's loss in the event of foreclosure. Historically that has worked out to about 20 percent of the purchase price. In the back of a lender's mind is the thought that, with a fifth of the price put up by the borrower, the chance of default is very low. The buyer simply has too much to lose.

Therefore, be aware that in asking for 100 percent financing, you are asking a lender to loan you money with a very low assurance of commitment on your part. The lender's risk skyrockets, while the assurance of reward dips dramatically as you approach a 100 percent Loan to Value (LTV) ratio. Of course, you can up that assurance dramatically by moving into the property yourself. Becoming an owner-occupant instead of just an investor reduces the risk dramatically in a lender's mind, resulting in far better loans.

Thus, if you're an investor, you may find that an institutional lender such as a bank or a savings and loan will only give you a mortgage for a maximum of 80 to 90 percent LTV. On the other hand, if you'll be an owner-occupant, the lender may offer you a mortgage as high as 100 percent and, in some circumstances, may offer you extra money to help with the fix-up. This is a big reason so many people who buy fixer properties make it a point to live in those properties as well.

CAUTION

Some people tell the lender they intend to do one thing and then do another. They may intend to move in, but then circumstances change and they sell instead. The consequences can be dire.

Don't "Say" You'll Move in Unless You Intend To

Some people are tempted to claim they'll move to get great financing, although they really don't intend to. While circumstances can certainly change, it's never a good idea to deceive a lender. For one thing, most are pretty savvy and have a good idea what's going on. For another, the federal government can investigate a suspected falsified loan application and can prosecute if it finds evidence of fraud.

Don't take a chance. Do the right thing. Tell the truth on your application. If you can move in, do so. It may mean getting a mortgage that will allow you to do the deal at an interest rate you can afford. But, if you can't move in, don't say you can. In the long run, you'll get yourself into more trouble than it's worth.

You Need "Double" Financing

Keep in mind that normally you really need two kinds of loans with a fixer. You need a mortgage with which to buy the property initially. Then you need a mortgage or some other type of financing to pay for repairs. By combining these two types of financing, you sometimes can get institutional lenders to foot the entire bill.

Let's consider a rejuvenator property that Lou purchased. While it was cosmetically okay, it was old and needed updating. It needed a new heating system and plumbing and electrical upgrades. Lou felt that, given the neighborhood and the climate, he also needed to add air-conditioning and put in a modern kitchen. Because of its obsolescence, Lou was able to purchase at a very low price. He felt that once he had upgraded the property, he could turn around and sell it for a substantial profit.

However, Lou needed a place to live. He was currently renting. Because the fixer property was cosmetically okay, he figured he could move in and then, over time, upgrade the systems while he lived there.

CAUTION

Building and safety departments are usually willing to give an owner-occupant a permit to do most kinds of work, provided you are living in the property yourself. (Sometimes they ask that you continue to live in the home for some period of time, perhaps 6 to 12 months after the work is finished.) On the other hand, they usually will not give you a permit to do this kind of work yourself if you're an absentee owner/investor. Rather, they will require that the work be done by licensed contractors—something to keep in mind.

Lou went to a local bank that offered mortgages for houses in his area. He asked the bank to design a special type of mortgage for him. First, it had to cover all (or much of) the purchase costs. Second, it also had to cover the costs of fixing up the property.

The lender, who was flexible (as many local lenders are), agreed. What they gave Lou was a short-term purchase-construction loan at a slightly higher interest rate than a standard permanent loan. A construction loan, as opposed to a permanent mortgage, pays out its funds in a number of installments, usually as work is done. For example, such a loan may have five or ten payments. You don't take out the money until you are ready to start a new task. For example, if you're ready to upgrade the bathroom, you need to buy fixtures, tile, paint, caulking, and so on. Of course, you also don't pay interest on the loan money until you get it.

Under his new loan, Lou would get a big payment that would help him purchase the house. Then he would get additional payments as he completed work on the property. The total loan amount (95 percent of value) was based not on the purchase price but on the estimated value of the property after the work was completed. What this meant was that the first payment covered almost the entire cost of purchasing the property, while subsequent payments covered the fix-up costs. Because Lou had figured a 15 percent profit in his calculations, the new purchase-construction loan, in effect, covered all of his expenses.

No, you won't find every lender willing to give you a purchase-construction loan on a fixer. But some lenders are willing to be creative. You may have to look hard, but it is possible. Look especially for local lenders—hometown banks, savings and loan associations (S&Ls), and mutual savings companies.

Special Low-Down, No-Down Government Programs

A variety of government-insured home rehabilitation programs may be worth your consideration. The two most prominent are FHA Title 1 and Section 203(k).

Under Title 1, the loan is just for the fix-up work. The maximum loan amount is $25,000, to be used for home improvement. For an owner-occupied property, the combined mortgages can be up to 100 percent of the property's value (combined mortgage(s) plus home improvement loan). The maximum term is 20 years, and the interest rate is competitive. Check *www.hud.gov* for more information.

Section 203(k) loans are primarily for rehabilitation of single-family homes. Since 1996, they have only been available for owner-occupants. Under the program, the borrower gets one loan both to acquire and fix up a property (as discussed previously). The amount of the mortgage is based on the projected value of the property after all the work is completed. In other words, it takes into account the cost of the fix-up work, not just the property's current condition.

The property must be a one- to four-unit structure (condos qualify) and at least a year old. The maximum loan cannot exceed the cost of the property plus fix-up work, or 110 percent of the property's anticipated value after fix-up.

Money is advanced to pay off the property, and the amount designated for fix-up is placed into an escrow account, then released as work is completed according to a plan created by the borrower and approved by the FHA. The maximum loan amount is the same as that for the 203(b) program, which varies by state and county.

For more information, check into *www.hud.gov.* There are other restrictions and conditions on these loans, and they sometimes can be a nightmare to get because of the need to get appraisals and properly fill out documentation. Some lenders specialize in procuring them. If you go after one of these, be sure that your lender is experienced in the area.

Lenders Fannie Mae (*www.fanniemae.com*) and Freddie Mac (*www.freddiemac.com*) offer similar programs, sometimes with financing above 100 percent of the property's value. There are also a host of local state, city, and municipal programs.

Get the Seller to Cover 100 Percent of Your Financing

The seller can be a great source of financing. The trouble is that the vast majority of sellers want to get their cash out or are in no position to finance your purchase.

Occasionally, however, you'll find a seller who owns a property free and clear or who owes just a small amount. With the right amount of convincing, you might be able to get this seller to finance your purchase of the property. Here's how investor Lou did it.

Lou found a small cottage by the beach that had been on the market a long time. The Salinases, retirees, owned the place and wanted to sell it and move to the desert. It turned out that Salinases had a hefty retirement fund and really didn't need the cash from the sale. They just wanted out of the property. They didn't want the bother of renting it out and felt an obligation to stay in it until it was sold.

Because the land was near the beach, it was extremely valuable. The cottage itself was old, dilapidated, and—in Lou's opinion— worthless. The deal was a scraper.

Lou quickly learned that financing the purchase from institutional lenders, such as banks or savings and loans, would be hopeless. Most wouldn't lend at all because the value was in the lot, not the building. Those that would lend were only willing to lend a maximum of 70 percent of the purchase price. Further, most said they wouldn't subordinate (make their loan secondary) to the new construction loan Lou needed to put up a new house.

So Lou offered this proposal to the Salinases. The Salinases would give Lou 100 percent financing on the purchase of the property. In essence, they would turn it over to Lou. Further, the Salinas would agree to subordinate their mortgage to a new construction loan.

Lou would then get a construction loan; scrape the existing cottage off the property; and put up a beautiful, large new home and sell it. At the time of the sale, Lou would pay off the Salinases, the seller.

The Salinases considered the proposal. But, because they weren't born yesterday, they asked some questions. "What if we do this deal and then something happens to you and you don't put up the new house? You could get sick. Or some other, better financial deal could come up. Where would we be then? Maybe we could foreclose, but our house would be gone!"

Lou thought about it and told the Salinases that, given its condition, it probably would be easier to sell an empty lot than the lot with the old cottage on it, and an empty lot would probably fetch the same money. The Salinases would be taking a risk, but Lou pledged that he would do the work if it were humanly possible. He then showed them his track record of seven previous, similar jobs.

Mr. Salinas nodded, then asked, "But, what if you do put up the house and it's lovely, but the market is bad? Or the house turns out to cost too much for the area? What if you just can't sell it? We'd end up with a big house and a big construction loan on which we couldn't make the payments. Wouldn't we be in real trouble then?"

Lou had to agree that the Salinases were asking some shrewd questions. He also had to acknowledge that the Salinases would be at risk by doing this deal. They'd be at risk when the lot was cleared, during construction, and until the new home sold. Lou then asked if they would be willing to do the deal if they received a percentage of the profits. In other words, would the risk be worthwhile if the rewards were high enough?

Mr. and Mrs. Salinas considered. They said that, at the very worst, even if they lost the property completely, they would still have Mr. Salinas's retirement and be okay. On the other hand, if they could make a bigger profit on the deal, they'd like to do that instead. "What do you have in mind?" they asked Lou.

Lou suggested the following. He would do the deal, scrape the cottage, put up the house, and sell it. In addition to the sales price, Lou would show the Salinases all his costs and then his profit. He would then give the Salinases 20 percent of his profits.

Mr. Salinas chuckled and said he wasn't born yesterday. "No disrespect, young man, but there's no way I could know whether the numbers you were showing me were true or false." Then Mr. Salinas made a proposal. He suggested that Lou pay 20 percent more for the property up front and do the same deal. The risks were still the same to the Salinases, yet they'd get their extra reward beforehand.

Lou thought that over, but decided that a 20 percent increase in the purchase price of the property was much more than 20 percent of the profits later on. They dickered and finally compromised at 13 percent.

The Salinases and Lou did the deal, the house was scraped, a new one was put up, and it was sold. Lou paid the Salinases and the construction loan lender, kept a nice profit, and went off to find a new deal. The Salinases went off to retire in the desert, and Lou, as far as I know, is still doing fixer deals in the same area.

RULE

Yes, you can get 100 percent financing from a seller. But, unless the seller is a total fool, you'll have to give up some of your profits to get it.

With seller financing, you may end up giving up a percentage at resale or initially paying more for the property. In our example, the Salinases generously agreed to give 100 percent financing. In most cases, the seller will insist on your putting some cash into the deal.

Nevertheless, seller financing—up to 100 percent seller financing—is not only possible but the best possible way to handle many deals.

Are There "Special" Loans for Fixers?

The type of loan you're looking for will dictate the kind of lender you're looking for. If your fixer is bare land (the hardest collateral to use), I suggest you try only a bank or private individual. If you need a construction loan, approach a bank or possibly a savings and loan. If you need a standard mortgage, however, then you have at least the following sources:

- Banks
- Savings and loans (now sometimes called mutual banks)
- Mortgage brokers or bankers
- Commercial credit companies
- Credit unions (you must be a member)
- Local lenders (look under "Mortgages" in the phone book)
- Noninstitutional sources such as the seller (discussed earlier in this chapter) or private lenders (discussed next)

Are Private Lenders Out There?

Dealing with private lenders is an often-overlooked strategy. Private lenders are individuals (or sometimes corporations) who are willing to make high-risk loans for big potential rewards. Because of the terms they demand, most of us in real estate prefer not to use them unless absolutely necessary.

While a conventional lender may ask, for example, 6 or 7 percent interest, a private lender may want 8 or 9 percent. A conventional lender may want 2 points (a point is 1 percent of the loan amount) to make the loan; a private lender may want 5 points.

If a conventional lender is unwilling even to consider you because of spotty credit or the property selected, a private lender may consider any and all properties. On the other hand, most private lenders will not lend more than 80 percent of the current appraised value and frequently prefer to lend closer to 66 percent.

Using a private lender, in my opinion, should only be done in times of absolute necessity—when you want the place but you can't get financing anywhere else. In that case, then, figure out the cost, make sure you can afford it, and go for it. Better a tough lender than none at all.

Credit Cards to the Rescue

Finally, don't overlook the possibility of using your credit card or a personal line of credit for financing. Some credit card companies as of this writing charge as little as 7 to 10 percent interest on an introductory rate, although at the other end, some are charging an amazing 30 percent and higher for their weakest customers. A personal line of credit is an unsecured debt that some banks will extend to creditworthy customers.

However, be aware that you should arrange for both credit cards and lines of credit before you begin work or make the purchase. Once you're involved in a fixer project, you may have other financing that will interfere with your ability to obtain new credit. (Remember: Lenders don't like to give credit to anyone who they think may actually need it.)

CAUTION

If you're going to use credit cards, be sure you understand that these are for *short-term* borrowing, perhaps for a few months at most. You should have a plan (refinancing, selling, and so on) to pay them off before borrowing. Their high interest rates make them impractical for long-term borrowing.

Don't Forget to Check Your FICO Score

Today, virtually all institutional lenders rely on credit scoring (a way of numerically grading your creditworthiness). The higher your credit score, the easier you'll get a mortgage.

The basic credit score comes from FICO (Fair Isaac), although the major credit bureaus (Experian, Transunion, and Equifax) use their own versions. (The three main credit bureaus are now offering a "vantage" score that competes with FICO.) The scores generally run between 350 and 850. According to FICO, the average score in the United States is around 723. Scores above 640 are usually good enough for a prime mortgage (those with the lowest interest rates). Scores above 800 are "golden." To find your score, you can contact *www.myfico.com*—the fee is around $15. Credit reports themselves can be obtained free from each agency once a year from *www.annualcreditreport.com*.

The Mortgage Process

Regardless of where you apply, mortgage application forms are often the same (usually a standard form that secondary lenders such as Fannie Mae or Freddie Mac accept). Fill out your application. If you're going to apply to more than one lender, make copies. Just fill in the information from the old form, or use it, when making subsequent loan applications.

After reviewing your application, your lender will obtain a credit report on you, including your FICO score. You provide documentation of your income and bank balances. The lender arranges to have the property appraised. If everything checks out, you get the mortgage. If it doesn't, you look elsewhere.

Are Second Mortgages an Option?

These are mortgages that institutional lenders and sellers often give when there's already a first mortgage on the property that you're buying. The terms vary with second mortgages, although institutional seconds are typically for 5 to 15 years. They may either be at a fixed rate or at an adjustable rate.

If you get this loan after you've bought the property, it is commonly called a home equity loan, and the money can be used for almost any purpose. You must have equity in the property at least equal to the loan sought to get this type of loan. Usually lenders are hesitant to give a home equity loan until at least six months have passed since the owner purchased the property. However, if you can demonstrate that you have the equity, either because you put a lot of money down or the property has significantly appreciated in value, you can often get this type of loan earlier.

For more information on real estate financing, I suggest you check into my *Tips and Traps When Mortgage Hunting*, 3rd edition (McGraw-Hill Publisher, 2005).

Getting a Fixed Rate Mortgage versus an Adjustable Rate

Thus far, we've been talking about obtaining any mortgage. However, as soon as you're out there looking for a loan, you'll come up against the fixed-rate versus the adjustable-rate mortgage (ARM) dilemma. Which is better for you when doing a fixer?

To find out, you need to know some basics about both types. A fixed-rate mortgage is just that. Its interest rate does not vary during the life of the loan. For you, this means that you'll know exactly what your payment is month after month.

With an adjustable-rate mortgage, the interest rate changes periodically according to an index such as the prime rate or what it costs banks to borrow funds from the U.S. Treasury. An ARM's rate may change periodically, up or down. An ARM also may have a ceiling on the interest rate.

The ARM Advantage

ARMs sometimes offer an advantage to fixer investors: a lower-than-market initial interest rate (sometimes also called a "teaser"). If you plan to keep the property only a short time and then resell, why not get a mortgage with a low initial interest rate? Even if a property takes a longer time to sell and the teaser rate expires, it will take a considerable amount of time for your total interest payments to equal what you would have paid with a fixed-rate mortgage. Beware, however, of getting stuck with a high-interest ARM over the long-haul.

To evaluate an ARM, you need to understand "steps," "adjustment periods," "indexes," "margin," and "negative amortization." The following is a primer on adjustable rate mortgages.

Arm Primer

Steps. If you go for an ARM with a teaser, carefully check out the steps (the interest rate movement) and the adjustment periods (the time between each step). ARMs all have limitations on the maximum amount that the interest rate can move up or down in any given period. For example, your ARM may have steps of 1 percent. This means that in each adjustment period, the interest rate can go up or down a maximum of 1 percent.

Adjustment periods. When getting an ARM, what you ideally want for stability is a mortgage with very low steps and very long adjustment periods. I suggest never getting steps larger than 1 percent. If possible, get maximum steps of 0.5 to 0.75 percent. At the same time, negotiate long adjustment periods—six months or longer.

Indices. Your index is what your interest rate is tied to. It could be Treasury bill yields, the 11th Federal Reserve District cost of funds, the London Interbranch Borrowing Rate (LIBOR), or another reported figure. You want an index that won't shoot up quickly, taking your interest rate with it. Have the lender show you the ten-year history of the applicable index.

Margin. The margin is the difference between the index and the interest rate you are charged. You want a fair margin, one that brings the interest rate up to market, not higher than market.

Negative amortization. Some mortgages have a cap or maximum amount that the *payment* rises each adjustment period but no cap on the *interest rate*. The result is that interest due but not paid on the mortgage is added to the principal. You can end up owing more than you borrowed! Never think that you'll be reselling before the lack of a cap can hurt you. The possibility that you'll have to keep the property should be built into your deal. Such a possibility means you'd never take a mortgage with negative amortization.

What about Assuming an Existing Mortgage?

Some mortgages taken out before the 1990s can be assumed or taken over. The advantage to the new mortgage holder is that you get the old interest rate and terms.

Two types of assumable loans are available today. The first type is government-guaranteed or insured loans, such as VA and FHA mortgages. The second is ARMs, most of which are assumable, but only if you qualify at the current market rate.

VA and FHA loans are no longer freely assumable, as they were in the past. Depending on when they were placed on the property, you may need to submit an application and credit report to assume them.

The advantage of an assumption is the reduced cost. An old FHA or VA loan may sometimes have a much lower interest rate. This makes it a good assumption possibility. The problem is that usually an older loan is written for substantially less than the purchase price. In other words, it isn't a big enough mortgage. If you don't have enough cash to pay the difference, in addition to the assumption, you also may need to get a second, new mortgage either from an institution or the seller.

ARMs usually are assumable and may have large enough balances to be worthwhile, because they are usually fairly recent loans. However, with an ARM, you get the current market rate and you have to qualify fully. The advantage, however, is that the cost of assuming the loan—points, title insurance, etc.—is usually greatly reduced compared to getting a new loan. Thus, assuming an ARM might be to your advantage.

What If You Have Credit Problems?

Many books on the market purport to tell you how to fix credit problems. The truth is that, if you have a credit problem, you have only two options: either you have to find a way to get the blemish removed from your credit, or you must find a lender who is willing to ignore the blemish and still give you a mortgage (such as with the seller mortgages described above). Here are some hints in both areas.

Helping Bad Credit Reports

Generally speaking, the only way you can get a bad report removed from your credit history is to have the source call or write the credit reporting agency and tell them to take it off. Or, if the bad report is a mistake, contact the credit bureau, and it will give you the procedure for correcting the error.

Why would a lender write your credit bureau? They may have made a mistake (as opposed to the credit bureau). Mistakes in credit reporting are legend. You could have paid the bill and the payment might not have been noted. Or the bad credit report could be for someone else. Be sure you correct an error, because it can continue to come back and haunt you. If you can't get the bad report removed by the source for whatever reason, at least insist that the credit reporting agency include a letter of explanation from you. Often, you are allowed to have such a letter noted. Be sure you explain the extenuating circumstances.

Helping Wary Lenders

If you know your lender will get a bad credit report on you, take the bull by the horns and deal with it up front. I had a friend with terrible credit. It came about because she was living with a fellow who used, then abused her credit. He charged all sorts of things on her credit and never paid for them. When she found out about it, they had a fight and he left. But by that time, she had not a chance in the world of paying off the large balances.

When she applied for a mortgage, she included a letter of explanation, noting that this had all occurred some three years earlier and that, prior to that time and since, she had perfect credit. The first lender she went to turned her down. But the second accepted the explanation and moved forward on the mortgage.

Can You Get Other People to Put Up Capital?

Finally, you can explore getting someone else to put up the capital for your fixer project. Quite frankly, your best chance of getting the money you need with nothing more than a handshake is from your parents, siblings, or other close relatives. Assuming that over the years, you've convinced them of your financial acumen and your strong feelings of responsibility toward repaying a debt, they may be more than happy to give you a personal loan.

CAUTION

Lenders are like elephants: They never forget bad credit. At all costs, try to avoid late payments on a mortgage or, the ultimate worst, a foreclosure. Lenders hate lending money to anyone who hasn't kept up their mortgage, no matter the reason.

Quite frankly, I believe close friends are the least likely to lend you money. They may be competitive with you, jealous of your accomplishments, and scornful of your failures. You can try, but don't be surprised if you come up empty-handed.

Then, of course, you can approach associates. Members of your dream team, coworkers, and social acquaintances (but not close friends) may be willing to put up the capital you need. Present the deal as a straight loan and, I believe, you're less likely to get the money (though if you do, your profit will be higher). Associates are likely to want a piece of the action. Your best chance of getting them to put up money is to present the deal as an investment opportunity.

Finally, some venture capitalists make a business of lending money to small and large businesses. However, to attract these people, you will probably need to borrow a large sum and will need a written proposal or plan. Venture capitalists are a world unto their own, and I don't suggest you consider them until you have a $1 million minimum project, a strong track record of success, and a business plan that simply cannot be denied.

As we noted at the beginning of this chapter, financing is the name of the game in real estate. Those who get it have the best opportunity to move forward with purchases and with fixing up property. Those who don't secure financing are often left out of the fixer playing field.

10 Getting Sellers to Accept Lowball Offers

To get a good deal for yourself, you must offer a price that will allow you to pay for repairs, earn a profit, and offer the property for resale at a price buyers will be willing to pay. The seller may think your offer to purchase is insultingly low—a lowball offer. But pay too much, and you'll be making the seller very happy but disappointing yourself.

Here's how to get your "lowball" offer accepted.

Negotiating a Deal

If you've ever tried to buy a fixer, you'll appreciate the following true story. Sidney and Leslie wanted to buy a house in a good neighborhood which, unfortunately, also had higher prices. The couple simply couldn't afford a home that was in good shape, so they looked for a cosmetic fixer, one with a lower price that needed simple work they could handle.

RULE

Buy the highest-value fixer you can afford. It won't cost much more to fix up than a lower-priced property, but you'll have a bigger budget to work with and more profit when you resell.

Eventually, after nearly four months of searching, they located an old, two-story house that had fallen into disrepair. The plumbing and electrical systems seemed up to snuff, but the house needed a new furnace, complete repainting inside and out, and many new fixtures. It had been a rental, and the tenants had not been kind to it.

The owner lived across the state and said, via his agent, that he was anxious to sell but gave no specifics. So Sidney and Leslie made what they considered a reasonable offer. After checking out the property and doing their homework (as described in Chapter 5), they offered $275,000, $75,000 less than the owner was asking.

The owner was outraged. He said that homes in the area regularly sold for $350,000 and more. Sidney and Leslie's low offer was nothing more than an attempt to steal the property. But he then countered at $300,000—$50,000 less than he had been asking!

Sidney and Leslie were tempted. They wanted the house for more than just fixing up; they wanted it to live in, hopefully for a long time. However, they simply couldn't afford to pay the $300,000 plus the costs of fixing it up so it would be ready to move in. Their offer of $275,000 was what they could afford, and they said so through their agent.

The owner said he wanted a couple of weeks to think about it. If they'd leave the offer open-ended, he'd let them know.

They refused. They gave him 24 hours to decide. If his answer was no, they would look elsewhere.

The owner countered again at $290,000, then yet again at $285,000. Eventually, he agreed to Sidney and Leslie's $275,000 offer, provided they could close the deal in 30 days, which they just managed to do.

Why Was the Deal Made?

It's nice to hear stories about how people successfully pay low-ball prices for a good fixer property. However, if you're going to duplicate what was done here, it's important that you understand the story behind the story. Why was the seller willing to drop the asking price $75,000?

Appearance. As noted in Chapter 2, cosmetic fixers can be some of the worst-appearing properties. Typically they need paint and have holes in the walls, broken windows, missing or destroyed appliances, and ravaged yards. They just look bad. Hence, it's hard to get 95 percent of buyers even to consider them. Usually, the only people who will make offers are those looking for a fixer.

Absentee owner. Our buyers knew the owner lived across the state. It would be difficult for him to supervise the cleaning and fixing the house needed. To get it done, he'd have to hire a crew and trust them to do the work. Further, during this time, the home would be difficult to sell. Finally, if the workers did a half-baked job, the house still wouldn't look good and might be even harder to sell, much less for a good price. In other words, the owner's fix-up options were limited.

Unrealistically high asking price. The owner realized that the property was overpriced. He and his agent knew that similar properties in good shape were selling for "more than $350,000." The owner had already prepared himself to take much less because of his rundown property. It's important to remember that, very often, a seller will know what a house is worth yet still will ask con-siderably more, hoping to get a foolish buyer to pay the higher price.

Persistent, confident buyers. Our buyers, Sidney and Leslie, hung tough. They didn't respond to the owner's attempts to get them to bump up their price. They didn't fall for the "open-ended offer" ploy, which would have meant that the seller could hold onto their offer while hoping and waiting for another, better offer to come in. An open-ended offer also would mean they couldn't make an offer on another property, because if this seller accepted their offer, they would be legally bound to complete the sale, and they couldn't afford to buy two houses.

Seller's motivation. Perhaps the biggest factor of all was the motivation of the seller. Sidney and Leslie discovered through a mutual friend that the seller had inherited the house from an uncle who had died a few years earlier. The seller simply wanted to get his cash out. He didn't want to be an absentee landlord, and he didn't want to fix up the property. He just wanted his cash, and he wanted it as soon as possible.

In the above example, we've seen how circumstances, property condition, and the right buying stance can allow you to purchase a fixer at a price you believe is fair. These factors all worked for Sidney and Leslie. A less-motivated seller might have found other alternatives than dropping his price more than 20 percent.

RULE

Find out *why* the seller wants out, and you'll be halfway toward getting your lowball offer accepted.

How Do You Discover the Seller's Motivation?

If you need to know a single overriding fact when attempting to get a lowball offer accepted, it's why the seller has the property on the market. How do you find out? One good way is just to ask. Even though the seller was out of town, Sidney and Leslie could easily have gotten his phone number through property tax records. They could even have driven to see him. They could have shown up to present their offer or one of their counteroffers. Or earlier on, they could have dropped in as potential buyers interested in his property. Rarely will a seller turn away a serious buyer.

That's why I advise speaking directly to the seller. Always ask this point-blank question: "Why are you selling?"

Most times, it has been my experience that the seller gives an honest (or near-honest) answer. The seller in our example might have mentioned that he inherited the house and didn't want to bother with it. If I were the seller, I wouldn't have mentioned just how anxious I was to dump the place, but in a direct meeting, a seller often may admit this as well. The best and quickest way you have of finding out the seller's motivation is simply to ask.

You can also ask others. You can ask the agent (who may or may not know or be candid). You can ask tenants and neighbors who may know (or who may *think* they know).

Finally, you can judge by what the seller does. If the seller counters with a big cut in the selling price (as was the case here), you have a pretty good idea that they're anxious. A seller who is not anxious will often counter at a price very close to the original, hoping that your lowball offer was just a trial balloon. A desperate seller, however, won't want to lose you and will try to get as close to your offer as possible to keep you hooked.

Try the "Home Inspection" Gambit

In today's market, it's almost a necessity to have a home inspection prior to the conclusion of the sale. Buyers want it so that they have a better idea of what they're purchasing. Sellers prefer it because it helps them after the sale to mitigate the buyer's complaints about problems with the property. If the buyer says, for example, "I never would have bought this property if I'd known it had a bad roof," the seller can respond, "You had it inspected. Blame your inspector, not me."

There are many ways to use the home inspection as leverage, but here's the most common. The buyers, who are looking for a fixer, find a house and proceed to inspect it themselves. They determine just how much they can offer, then approach the seller to find out the seller's motivation.

They discover that the seller is not highly motivated. If the house doesn't sell this month, the seller figures it will sell next month or even next year. This sort of seller is not usually willing to come down much on price.

Now the buyers have to decide whether to make their best lowball offer for the property "as is" or offer something higher and hope that the inspection will reveal damage that the seller may not be aware of. Then they can renegotiate a lower price based on the inspection.

Offering the Lowball Price

Our buyers may offer their best lowball price. They may write into the contract that they agree to buy "as is" and even waive the right to an inspection. You'd better be pretty darn sure you found all the problems and that your guesstimates and those of your associates—see Chapter 8—are accurate before going this route. The reason is that once you buy it "as is," it's all yours, problems and all.

If the house has a lot of damage, the seller may find this lowball offer particularly appealing. Here are buyers who are making an offer and standing by it, regardless of the condition of the property. There aren't many buyers like this anymore. If I were a seller, I'd think three times before turning down or countering such an offer.

Raise Your Offer and Use Inspection to Renegotiate

The buyers can offer a higher price—one the seller is more likely to accept—but insist on an inspection. After the seller accepts, and when the inspection comes in revealing a lot of problems with the property, the buyers can then attempt to negotiate a lower price.

If you use this method, be sure that you make the purchase contingent on your approval of the inspection. In other words, if you don't like what the inspection report says (regardless of what it says), you aren't committed to make the purchase.

Pros and Cons of Each Method

While the first method is more straightforward, it's less likely to snare a truly unmotivated seller. The seller may simply say that while your offer is appealing because you're accepting the house "as is," it's simply too low. This seller has the time to wait, hoping for a better offer to come by.

On the other hand, while the second method is disingenuous at worst, it's more likely to get results, because it forces the seller to consider the property's true problems. Potential buyers have made an offer to purchase, contingent on an inspection. But, once the inspection reveals the property's true terrible shape, they are only willing to buy at a reduced price. Even an unmotivated seller, in this second case, is likely to see that the price must be lowered because of the property's condition.

Which Arguments Should You Use?

The problem with getting sellers to accept lowball offers is that they just don't want to feel they are losing money. Even if the lowball offer is four times what they paid for the property years ago, if it's less than nearby homes are going for, they just don't want to consider it. Many sellers would rather pass up a good offer than accept it, if they believe they would get less money than their neighbors who sold homes recently. So your task as a fixer buyer is to convince sellers that their best interest lies in accepting your offer.

Arguments to Get a Lower Price

Condition. The first step in any negotiation over a fixer is to get consensus on the condition of the property. If you say it's run-down and a mess, but the seller says it looks fine, the deal is hopeless. You won't get anywhere in negotiations over price until the seller agrees with you about the condition of the property. How do you get an uncompromising seller to be realistic? Consider using the home inspection gambit discussed previously. If you can't get the seller to accept the fact that no sane person will buy that property at full, great-shape price, get out of there and move on to the next property. You can't reason with a fool.

It costs a lot to fix up. Once the seller agrees with you that the house is in terrible condition and acknowledges that a discount is in order, the only remaining question is: How big a discount? Bring out the figures you've developed and explain them in detail. If an associate is donating some work, point that out. Point out all the work you're doing and not directly charging for. In short, show the seller how much fixing up the property will cost you. Get the seller to acknowledge that your figures are reasonable. (They had better be, or else you could lose money on the job.)

Compare your fixing up the property to the seller's fixing it up. Remember, if the seller fixes up the property, they will have to spend time, perhaps months or even a year, fixing up the place. During that time, the seller may not be able to live in the house and almost certainly will not be able to rent it out. Further, current mortgage payments, taxes, insurance, and other costs will continue to run. Finally, ask if the seller can afford to pay the costs. Usually fixing up means the person doing the work has to get financing to cover it. A new mortgage is not unusual. Can the seller get this financing? Does the seller want to? Further, point out how much fixing up the property realistically will cost the seller in time and money. And then what will the seller gain? After it's all fixed up, the seller still must find a buyer. And once that buyer is found, the price received probably won't be far off from what you are offering *plus* the costs of fixing it up. In short, the seller can save time, money, and effort simply by selling to you now . . . and still realize the same amount as if they held on, fixed up, and sold later!

The hassle. I always ask sellers point-blank if they have ever done any fix-up work. Have they waited a half-day, a day, a week, or more for a worker or subcontractor to show up, only to have the person come in, do a few hours of labor and then leave with that job still unfinished? It happens all the time. What about work going on while they're trying to live in the property? There's always dust. The rain and dirt manage to come in. There's the noise. And don't think that because the tradespeople promise they'll only be at the job from 9:00 AM to 5:00 PM, they'll stick to those hours. Expect them to show up at 7:00 AM and not leave until 9:00 PM. Yes, of course, they'll say they'll do your job when you want it. But then they may not show up at all! Most sellers have had at least a bit of experience with having work done for them and, once reminded, should quickly remember just how unpleasant it was. Keep reminding them of the hassle every time they get back to the high price they want.

These are the arguments you can use to get sellers to lower their price to something you're willing to pay. Will these arguments work every time? Certainly not. But, if you're convincing, they should work often enough to get you the properties you want at the prices you want to pay.

Arguments to Get a Lower Price for a Fixer

- The property needs fixing up, and price is directly related to the condition of the property. Fix-up costs are high.
- Someone has to fix it up, and the costs for everybody will be roughly the same.
- The sellers can avoid the hassle of fixing it up by selling at a realistic price now.

Rules for Getting Your Price

- Be reasonable
- Treat the whole matter as business
- Never take negotiating personally
- Don't ask for favors—make the sellers see what's best for them

11 Turn the Seller into a Partner

Have you ever gone looking for a fixer and found a great property, only to discover that the sellers are unreasonable about the price? Yes, they want to sell. But they're convinced that the property is worth far more, even in its present condition, than you're willing or able to offer.

If you've spent any time at all looking for fixers, I'm sure you've run into this situation. If you have, then you've probably done what I and most others do. Chalk it up to experience and keep looking.

Sometimes, however, there's an alternative that can work with uncompromising sellers: make them a partner. In Chapter 8, we introduced the idea of using partnerships to get financing. Now, we'll expand partnership into something more formal. Remember, sometimes sellers can only come to terms with what their property is worth when they actually see what has to be done, see the work being done, and then realize the costs involved. Nothing is more convincing than actually doing the fix-up work.

Of course, most times sellers don't want to be bothered with this. They just want a clean sale. They want to get their money out of the property so they can move on and leave the headaches to you. Other times, however, sellers simply can't sell this way so they may be willing to listen to reason.

A Shared Fixer?

Sam had a two-story Victorian house in San Francisco. The building was 80 years old and needed both cosmetic work as well as rejuvenation. The exterior needed new sheathing and a roof; the inside needed plastering and restaining of the extensive woodwork. A new heating system and work on the drains, as well as updating baths and the kitchen, were in order. Alice wanted to buy and fix the place, but she realized the work needed was extensive and expensive. She calculated that fixing up the property and getting her profit out of it would cost close to $200,000. (Fixers of this magnitude are not unusual near San Francisco, where housing prices are among the highest in the nation.)

Sam, however, was stuck on asking a price that was only $100,000 less than what the house would sell for if completely refurbished. There was a $100,000 difference between what Alice was offering and what Sam was willing to sell for; they were a veritable ocean apart.

When Alice talked with Sam, however, she quickly learned that she wasn't the first person to differ with him on this. He had had the house on the market for a long time, and numerous other investors had come by, wanting to fix it up. All of their estimates had been in about the same ballpark. Sam was just plain stubborn.

So Alice gave him this proposal: Why not work with her to fix up the property and then sell it when it was refurbished? A completed fixer in the neighborhood should be a cinch to sell. That way, Sam would know exactly how much fixing up the place cost and for how much it ultimately sold. He could share in the profits.

Sam thought it was the best idea since sliced bread. He jumped at the chance to do it. Alice told him, "Whoa, we have to set up the ground rules so that neither of us gets hurt on the deal." Here's what Alice proposed:

- Sam would share ownership of the property with Alice.
- Alice would secure added financing to do the fix-up work and see that it was all done properly.
- After the work was done, they would call in a professional appraiser to tell them what it was worth, and they would list it for that amount.

When the place was sold, Alice would take 10 percent of the sales price as her share of the profit. Out of the balance, all costs of the sale, including the commission, as well as the mortgages on the property would be paid. What was left would be Sam's share.

For Alice, the deal was very sweet. To begin with, she wouldn't have to come up with any down payment or arrange any purchase money financing. She was simply getting half-ownership in the property directly from Sam.

Of course, she would be responsible for getting financing to do the work and getting it done right. Sam insisted on a clause specifying that, if she backed out on this, the ownership would immediately revert back to him alone.

Finally, Alice's profit was almost guaranteed, as long as the house eventually sold. She figured it would sell in the $900,000-plus range, which meant she'd make at least $90,000 on the deal. This return would probably be less than if she bought it outright, but then again, she wouldn't have to come up with any cash.

For Sam, it didn't sound like such a bad deal either. He was wary of the 10 percent profit to Alice, but agreed that she had to do a lot of work to get it, so it was probably fair. Further, he would watch closely to see that no more money was spent on the fix-up than absolutely necessary. As a result, his remainder would be:

Sales price – Costs of sale – Payoff of mortgages – Alice's 10%
= Sam's share

Sam was sure that his profit would be more than if he had sold it for what Alice offered in the first place. (As it ultimately turned out, it was just a tiny bit more.)

Keep in mind that all this worked out in large part because Sam had a lot of equity in the house. He could afford to be flexible about what he received, because he didn't have a big mortgage hanging over his head. This sort of deal won't work when the seller has just marginal equity.

Understanding Equity Sharing

The technique used in Sam and Alice's deal is called "equity sharing." This concept came into existence in the late 1970s, although for a different purpose. Back then, property was rapidly appreciating in all parts of the country. If you bought, you could assume that your home would go up in value a minimum of 10 percent a year. (That, of course, doesn't compare to the 20 percent or more price inflation we've seen in recent years in many areas.)

The problem was that then, as now, those who wanted to buy frequently couldn't afford to. They didn't have enough money for a down payment. On the other hand, sellers looking at the rapid price appreciation were not anxious to sell. They kept wondering about whether they should hold on to the property. Why sell something that was going up so rapidly in price? One answer was equity sharing.

Back then, the way it worked was that a buyer and seller would enter into an equity-sharing agreement. While the terms could vary enormously, generally they provided that the seller would throw in their equity and the buyer would move into the property; make the monthly payments for mortgage, taxes, and insurance; and maintain the place. Then, after a set period of time, typically a few years, the property would be placed on the market.

From the sale, the seller would get back their equity. Any balance—and there was usually a big balance given the price appreciation—would be split between the equity sharers. Many such arrangements were made and, while some didn't work out, many did, with both parties profiting handsomely.

While the terms are certainly different, it is possible to equity-share a fixer. You're the investor in this case, the party coming in who wants to buy the property. The seller is the one who shares. There are three reasons why you would want to equity-share a fixer:

1. The seller is unrealistic about the property'ys sales price in unrefurbished condition (as in our example).
2. You don't have the cash to buy the fixer outright.
3. You can't get the financing to buy the fixer outright.

If it turns out that any or all of the above reasons fit you, then you should at least consider the possibility of doing an equity-share with the seller. To do this, however, you'll have to sell the owner of the property on the concept.

Selling the Owner on Equity Sharing

You must demonstrate three qualities to convince the owner to join in an equity-share with you:

1. *Be honest.* You need to convince an owner/seller that you are completely honest. Sellers must believe that you will do what you say and not cheat them, or they will never go along with what you propose. How do you convince another person of your honesty? It's simple: Never exaggerate and never equivocate. When there's a problem or something comes up to your disadvantage, admit it. People judge us by how well we respond to adversity. If it turns out we were wrong in an honest mistake, do we admit it? If something occurs that could cost us money, do we try to hide the fact or bring it out in the open? I personally like to go out for lunch or coffee with a person with whom I'm going to work and just talk. We don't have to talk about anything in particular. But while we're talking, I listen carefully to what the other person says and judge their level of honesty. I might bring up a point that's disadvantageous (on the surface) for their position. How do they handle it? Do they hide it? Ignore it? Or acknowledge it? If you're forthcoming with sellers and they are reasonable (something that's essential for a sharing arrangement), they should be able to sense your honesty pretty quickly.
2. *Explain everything.* It's important that sellers understand what's involved in a shared-equity arrangement, both the good and the bad. Your partner needs to know up front what will happen if things go well and what will happen if they go badly. To make an informed decision, both the risks and rewards must be clearly outlined. You also need to dem-

onstrate that you are capable of handling the fix-up work. I don't encourage you to try sharing equity on your first fixer. Rather, you need a successful track record to help convince a seller to go along with a shared-equity proposal. Ideally, you should be able to point to half a dozen other properties you fixed up and sold for a profit. Or at least a few. Your track record helps establish your credibility in a seller's eyes.

3. *Show the advantages.* Finally, understand why sellers want to get rid of their properties and point out why doing an equity-share could be to their advantage. In our example with Sam and Alice, it turned out that Sam did not make significantly more money. However, in other situations, particularly when the fixer is in such rundown condition that a sale at almost any price is difficult, the deal could work out much better.

In short, you must present sharing equity as an attractive alternative. If the owner/seller agrees (and has sufficient equity), you're on your way.

CAUTION

Taking in a partner in any transaction is always risky business. You can't know that your partner will be as honest or as savvy as you. Your partner may try to cheat you or do something foolish that could cost you money. Therefore, you need to protect yourself as much as possible.

How Do You Protect Yourself?

To be successful, however, you must be sure that your interests are protected.

While there is no such thing as absolute protection, you can get assurance that you'll be okay in the deal by making all the terms very clear to everyone in a written agreement. Here are 11 requirements that I would consider *the absolute minimum* in any shared-equity agreement I signed. You may want or need additional terms.

1. *Written agreement.* This should be prepared by an attorney who is familiar with the equity-sharing concept and has done these before. Some real estate attorneys have ready-to-go forms that they can adjust to fit your specific situation. Don't attempt to create an equity-sharing agreement without an attorney's help.

2. *Ownership.* You must spell out clearly how the title to the property will be held during the fix-up period. Ideally, you would share title with the seller. However, to keep the current financing, it may be to everyone's advantage to have the seller keep title and for you to have a contract. If so, be sure that you are protected from the owner's selling out from under you to someone else. You might, for example, have all additional financing in the owner's name, so you wouldn't be liable for it. Or you may be able to have something, such as a contract of sale, recorded that protects your interest and prevents and easy sale without your approval.

3. *Time frame.* You need to be very specific about how long you will have to complete the fix-up work (allow yourself ample time) and when the house will be put up for sale. You don't want a situation where the owner keeps procrastinating about selling the property after it's fully fixed.

4. *Work to be done.* Be very clear about what work you plan to do, how you plan to do it, where the money is coming from (additional financing), and when you will finish. The seller needs to know these things to feel comfortable about the deal.

5. *Profits.* Be very clear about the profits. In our last example, Alice's profits came off the top. In other deals you may make, the seller may want to get their equity out, pay all costs, and then divide the remainder. Be sure to strike a deal that you feel is fair to you.

6. *Appraisal.* The value of the property at resale is critical. Be sure you're in agreement on some method for determining the resale price. For example, you could hire an independent

appraiser, or you could call in three real estate agents for their evaluations and then take an average of the three. You should also specify that the price will be reduced by a certain amount every three months, or some other term, if the property doesn't sell.

7. *Sale*. You need to specify how the property will be resold. Will you do it yourself, without an agent (FSBO)? If so, the sale could take longer. Or will you list it? With whom?

8. *Maintenance costs*. Someone will have to pay for the mortgage, taxes, insurance, and upkeep until the property resells. Who will that be? If it's you, how will you get your money back? If it's the owner, will these expenses be added to the owner's equity, which may come out of the deal first, or will these amounts be considered as costs of doing the deal?

9. *Occupancy*. Does the owner get to stay in the property while the work is being done? Do you? Will you rent it out? What about when the occupant must temporarily leave so some work such as wiring or plumbing can be completed?

10. *Decision not to sell*. What if one party doesn't want to sell? Agreements are great, but you or your partner's frame of mind when it's time to sell can be far different from when you entered into the agreement. What if the sellers decide that, rather than sell, the place came out so beautifully they'd like to live in it themselves? Or hold it as an investment rental? Your agreement should include detailed information on how one partner can buy out the other, including costs.

11. *Arbitration*. Finally, there's always the chance that you forgot to include something or that somewhere along the way a disagreement will arise. How will you deal with it? There's always the matter of court and lawyers. However, a more reasonable and less expensive approach may be arbitration. You and your partner may want to agree to arbitration in advance. However, if you do, be sure to specify how the arbitrator will be chosen. You may want to use a professional arbitrator, but be aware that this solution tends to be quite costly.

12 Fixing Up Multiunit Residential, Commercial, and Office Buildings

Don't get stuck only thinking inside the box. Yes, individual homes are a great place to start. Nearly everyone who's made money in fixers began there. Once you get your feet wet, however, there are all sorts of other possibilities.

Apartment Fixers

Apartment building prices fluctuate wildly. From about the late 1960s to the late 1980s, apartment buildings in many areas of the country went up in price. One reason was the general inflation in real estate values. Another was that it was possible to keep raising rents, and as long as rents went up, building valuations (which are based on income) went up as well. Finally, in some cases apartments were sold, fixed up, and then resold as condos. These were called "conversions."

From the late 1980s to the end of the 1990s, the nationwide real estate market slumped, and prices for apartment buildings leveled off and, in many areas, declined. At that point, you could have bought one of these buildings for a song.

After the turn of the century, however, prices for apartment and commercial buildings shot up in many areas. As long as prices rise, if you can find a building in bad shape and fix it up, you can make a significant profit. In many older areas of cities, fixer opportunities in apartment buildings abound. Note: Price appreciation for commercial and residential properties does not move in sync. Often one will be declining while the other is rising. Be sure to thoroughly evaluate the market.

For the enterprising individual, the challenge is to find one of these buildings, buy it, fill it with high-paying tenants, and sell it for amazingly high profits. It's being done today, and you can do it too.

How Do You Buy an Apartment Fixer?

What you need to do, as with a fixer house, is determine two values:

1. The ultimate value that the property will bring on resale after it's fixed up
2. The value you need to place on it now in order to be able to buy, fix up, and sell it for a profit

Generally speaking, you first determine the ultimate value and then determine your costs. Subtract your costs and your minimally acceptable profit from the resale value, and you have the maximum amount you can afford to offer. See Chapter 5 for the basic formula.

In addition to the rules for making lowball offers that we've already discussed (Chapter 10) and structuring the deal, you will want to keep in mind some special considerations when buying apartment buildings.

Special Considerations

True rental rate. As noted, value is based on rental income. A multiplier is often used; for example, the sale value may be ten times the annual rental rate. (Check with a good real estate agent for the current multiplier to use in your area.) If you have five units that rent at $1,000 per month each, you have $60,000 a year income and, multiplying by a multiplier of 10, a rough value of $600,000. What should be obvious is that you can't know how much the true value is until you know what the true rental rate is.

So spend some time finding out. Don't just ask for the rental income of the units you're buying. Chances are you can find similar units around. Check with their owners (or tenants) to see how much they rent for. If you don't know how much annual rental income to expect from your identified fixer, you'll never get an accurate price for the property.

True vacancy rate. Similarly, every area has a vacancy rate. Find out what that is for the building you are considering. Don't accept an owner's estimation that, "We figure about 5 percent for vacancies," or, "The property is never vacant— it rents up right away."

Again, check with apartment owners of nearby similar buildings. Most will be happy to tell you their vacancy rate. You may get the same information from a local apartment owner's association. The easiest way to locate it may be through its Web site, if it has one. Use a search engine such as Yahoo or Google and the key words *apartment, association, owners.* Small organizations may not have a phone number listed, but check the phone book anyway under "associations" or "apartments."

Finally, don't forget about the down time between rentals—the unit must be cleaned. This is not the same as fixing up the building. We're talking here of cleaning up after an old tenant moves out and before a new one can move in. Cleanup time sometimes depends on the size of the units and how new they are. (Is the carpeting new and easily cleanable? What about the appliances?) Also, is a tenant waiting to move in, or does reletting your units take months?

Rent control restrictions. Nothing will sink you faster than to learn, after a purchase, that the area has rental controls. These are set by local governments and essentially mean that you can't raise a tenant's rent except by a set (usually minimal) amount. Check this out with the appropriate local government agency, usually a rent control board or a building and planning department.

Keep in mind that sometimes, even in areas with rent control, when a tenant voluntarily moves out, the landlord may be allowed to raise the rent, even up to current market levels. Also, some allowance may be made when the building is sold.

Cleaning/security deposits. Find out who has these and how much they are. You don't want to buy an apartment building only to learn that the former owner kept thousands of dollars in deposits that tenants now expect you to return.

The location, amount, and disposition of deposits should be clearly spelled out in a written purchase agreement. Sometimes the deposits will be so high they can be a deal maker or a deal breaker.

If you're new to apartment ownership, you will have many other questions. We'll deal with some of these in the next section. In any event, you would be wise to consult with a savvy real estate agent in your area who deals strictly with these units. This agent can usually tell you more in a few minutes than you could learn in months of investigating this area for yourself.

Commercial Fixers

Commercial fixers follow a similar pattern to apartment buildings. They were hot until the late 1980s, then cooled off until the late 1990s, and now, in some areas, are hot again.

Before buying, be sure to check your area carefully for available commercial rental space. If it's tight, without much space available (as in most, but not all, areas of the country), it's a great time to jump in. Once you find a fixer and remedy it, you should have no trouble renting it out.

The Importance of Location

It's been said many times that location is the most important factor in real estate value. When it comes to *commercial* real estate, location becomes almost the *only* factor. It doesn't matter whether the property is a small strip shopping center, a large mall-type center, or office space—what will most determine success or failure is location.

Consequently, if you're interested in fixing up commercial real estate, the first thing that you need to do is to find run-down properties in great locations. In addition, contact commercial real estate agents. In larger real estate offices, typically one or two agents specialize in commercial properties. (Everyone else sells houses.) You need to contact these special agents. Also, some firms do nothing but commercial property.

When trying to evaluate the location for a commercial fixer, you need to look at this a bit differently than for residential property. What you should pay special attention to is "exposure." By this, I mean you need a good location on a heavily trafficked street. If it's office space, a good commercial location doesn't hurt. But being isolated on a side street (a killer for purely commercial) isn't always so bad for offices, if there is ample parking.

Also, pay special attention to the surrounding neighborhood, particularly with small strip malls. With a large building or mall, the commercial property, in essence, creates its own neighborhood environment. For a mall owner, the biggest concern often is being close to freeway off-ramps. With small strip shops or office buildings, however, you want to be near other, similar businesses so that the combined effect is to bring in more customers.

There also can be a downside to the neighborhood. Today, many older commercial and office buildings are in deteriorating neighborhoods with crime problems. The personal safety aspect could drive customers and tenants away. I never buy anything in a neighborhood where I'm afraid to walk in the evening.

You also need to be sure the commercial building has easy access from the street, so customers can get in, and that it has adequate parking. Finally, there's the matter of how the property looks to someone approaching it. It needs a nice appearance, or you may need to put up a new facade as part of your fixing up.

How Do You Get the Right Price?

Just as with any other property, you need to know your costs before you can determine the price you can offer. However, unlike with residential property, commercial property often has a design factor.

It has to look appealing to draw people in. Therefore, as part of determining your costs, you should consult with a good architect (perhaps a member of your dream team?) who can point out different ways to spice up the building.

Also, just as with apartment buildings, you want to get a good handle on how much you can reasonably expect for rents and what the vacancy rate is. Keep in mind that the rental and vacancy rates are often affected by the overall amount of space available. If too much space is available, landlords cut their rental rates to attract tenants. Thus, you can have no vacancies at a low rate or very high vacancies at a higher rental rate. You need to know what you're likely to experience in your projected area in the near future.

Special Considerations

Just as with apartment buildings, there are things to watch out for that are peculiar to commercial buildings. Here are a few to check out.

Lease terms. Check the leases of the current tenants. Commercial leases are significantly different from residential leases. With commercial property, you often want the tenant to pay not only the rent but the utilities and sometimes even the taxes and the insurance. "Net, net, net" leases, where the tenant pays all costs, are commonly used in these situations.

Some leases also provide that the rent is a minimum based on the gross (or net) sales of the tenant. As those sales increase, you get a percentage of them. These leases typically are found in large commercial developments.

Finally, you want to know the length of the leases. If the building is full, but those tenants have low-paying, long-term leases, you may want to pass on purchasing it. You could fix up the building and still not be able to raise rents and resell for a profit. As with apartment buildings, the value of commercial buildings is largely determined by income.

Perks. In commercial buildings, tenants sometimes will have perks. These could be certain reserved parking spots, the ability to use a walkway for tables (as with some restaurants), or having the tenant's name on a big sign facing the street. Sometimes these perks are understandable and reasonable. Other times, they inhibit your ability to fix up or even resell. You may have to check with each tenant separately to find out their perks.

Fix-up restrictions. Thus far, we've assumed no barriers to your fixing up a property. Usually there aren't. However, that can change significantly when it comes to commercial property.

I was once involved with a fairly large community shopping center that was nearly 30 years old. It was rundown and many of the stores were vacant, but it was in a great area with lots of parking and easy access. It was a perfect fixer. Or so I thought!

Then I learned that the city had passed resolutions requiring that, if any major work was done to a commercial center, the entire building had to be brought up to current city code. No sweat, right?

The problem is, they weren't just talking about things like electrical and plumbing. They were also talking about building design and landscaping. The current zoning code called for no signs facing the street—the "kiss of death" for many businesses.

The buildings also would have to be converted to a Spanish rustic architecture, then in vogue in the area. And a grass strip would have to be added between the sidewalk and the buildings, requiring major (read expensive) reconstruction work.

In short, bringing the shopping center up to current code would have cost millions more than the seller wanted as his asking price! Needless to say, I passed on the deal.

Be sure to check out any local government restrictions and regulations affecting a commercial center in which you may be interested. In particular, check with the local planning council and building and safety department. You may get a shock.

Toxic sites. You wouldn't buy a toxic site, you say? What if you didn't know it was toxic? These days, toxic sites aren't always what they seem to be. What if there once was a gas station on the land? Even though the station may be years gone, the tanks (or spillage from the tanks) may still be on or under the ground. Put your name on the deed, and you could end up responsible for the entire cleanup, which could cost thousands, hundreds of thousands, or millions of dollars—or more.

What if a small auto supply store used to be in the strip center you're considering? What if they dumped old oil and battery acid on the ground out back? Who do you think will be responsible for hauling dirt to a toxic dump site?

We're living in an era when we are increasingly conscious of protecting the environment around us, which is, of course, a great concept. We all want to breathe clean air and have healthy soil. But the flip side is that you can't afford to pay for someone else's earlier environmental mistakes and still make a profit.

Weather-associated problems. In some areas of the country the weather can be a factor in both the rental income and the aging of a property. In Phoenix, for example, don't expect a property to do a land office business in summer. When the weather is 115 degrees in the shade, people don't go out as much during the day and go only into air-conditioned buildings in the evening. If you planned on a year-round business and don't have air-conditioning, you could be in trouble.

Similarly, some areas in "mountain country" close up for three months, typically December, January, and February. The weather's too cold and conditions too treacherous for people to do any real business. If you buy in the summer and don't know about the winter, you could be in trouble.

Overview

Apartment and commercial buildings can offer rare fixer opportunities. If you want a challenge beyond the single-family house fixer, look to an apartment building or even a small strip mall. The risks and challenges are usually greater, but so are the potential rewards.

Fix It!

13   Quick Fixes

When it comes to fixers, most of us want to get in and out quick. The less expense, time, and effort involved, the better. That way we can take our profit and move on to the next project.

Sometimes a fixer won't cooperate, though, and we'll spend months, or even years, correcting serious problems. On the other hand, some fixers can be done quickly. The best example is the cosmetic fixer (described in Chapter 4).

With a cosmetic fixer, nothing's wrong with the house's basic structure; it just looks bad. The paint throughout may be old, dirty, or even peeling. The windows may be cracked. Sinks may be broken or missing. The carpet may be stained, torn, or worn out. The yard usually is totally run down with the lawn and shrubbery dead or dying. Typically, the cosmetic fixer is the worst-looking yet easiest to repair fixer you can find.

Little is seriously wrong with a cosmetic fixer. Fixing up, therefore, is mainly a matter of cleaning, painting, repairing, or replacing nonstructural items. This doesn't mean, however, that dealing with a cosmetic fixer is inexpensive or simple. You can lose money here just as fast as with a scraper, if you don't know what you're doing. In this chapter, we'll look at some tricks I've discovered over the years when dealing with the cosmetic fixer. The first part of this chapter will deal with what you should or should not clean and what's the best way to clean. The second part of the chapter will give tips on replacing items economically.

How Much Do You Need to Clean Up?

As noted, the typical cosmetic fixer is a mess. Very often, the previous owners either had rented the property out to tenants who almost destroyed it, or the owners went into foreclosure and took their anger and frustration out on the house. Thus, your first task is going to be cleaning up. In fact, you may not be able to see the total amount of repair work needed until the property is cleaned up.

My suggestion is that you hire someone else to do the basic clean up. People are available who do this professionally, and they are very inexpensive to hire. For example, a home I purchased to fix up had a very large yard, both behind and in front. The trees were overgrown, all kinds of trash had been dumped in the backyard (including the remains of an old Plymouth Barracuda!), and the front yard had weeds up to my waist. I could have rented a truck and spent a week (and earned a lot of backaches) getting rid of all of this stuff. Instead, I hired a crew whose ad I found in the local paper. They had their own large truck, and for $400 they trimmed, mowed, and cleaned everything up. And they did it all in one day!

The same applies to the inside. For around $250 for an average house, you should be able to hire a cleaning crew to come in and clean up bathrooms, kitchen, windows, and walls. They probably will take less than half a day and do a better job than you could do in three or four days. And they bring their own supplies.

Cleaning Carpets

You probably won't know the real condition of the carpeting until you've had the house cleaned up and the carpet at least vacuumed thoroughly. Once that's done, you need to decide whether you want a thorough carpet cleaning or to replace what's there. You'll want to check for stains, the condition of the nap—especially worn traffic patterns—and determine when replacing is better than cleaning. How to make this decision is discussed next.

Are dark-colored stains in areas that are likely to be out in the open (have no furniture)? For example, if you have a beige carpet in the living room and there's a red stain from some berry juice (something almost impossible to get out), you'll need to forget about cleaning and think about recarpeting at least that room.

On the other hand, if the carpet in the living room is okay, but some grease stains dot the carpet by the sliding glass door leading to the patio, you may want to have a thorough carpet cleaning done. Grease stains look bad, but with the powerful degreasers available today, they often will come out completely.

Ask someone who knows about cleaning carpets to tell you which stains will come out and which won't. Carpet cleaners will often come to your property to give you a bid. Avoid those who offer to clean for ridiculously low fees such as $15 a room. You won't get more than what you pay for. When a cleaner says they won't guarantee a stain will come out, they usually mean it won't come out. Save your money and don't clean—replace.

In addition to checking for stains, check the nap of the carpet. Look particularly in heavy traffic areas such as entrances to rooms and hallways. If the carpet is worn to the point where it's lying down and looks matted, again you're probably better off not cleaning it. You'll just have to replace it anyway. Cleaning will make a dirty carpet look better, but it won't make an old carpet look new. Besides, the cost of recarpeting may be far less than you imagine, as you'll discover later in this chapter.

Cleaning Walls

Cleaning walls is a no-no, except in kitchens and baths where a high-gloss paint is used. In living rooms, dining rooms, bedrooms, etc., where a flat, absorbent paint was used, stains on walls often cannot be easily cleaned off, particularly if the wall hasn't been recently painted. What happens is that the entire wall area gets dirty over time. When you scrub to remove a small stain, the newly clean area of the wall is now lighter than the remainder of the wall.

Now you must clean more of the wall to make things look even. Soon, you're trying to clean the entire wall, and the end result will be blotchy anyway. Keep in mind that with today's paints repainting a wall only takes a short time, usually much less time and effort than required to clean it.

On the other hand, I've had good success with spot repainting of walls, as long as the area to be touched up is fairly tiny and it's been less than a year since the wall was painted. Any longer than a year, and you run into a problem similar to that of cleaning dirt, described above.

Cleaning Tile

Tile will normally clean up very well with a strong cleaning agent. Grout between tiles, however, can be a different story. If it's white or light-colored and old, or very new, it will often absorb dirt and turn a mottled shade of brown.

Using a common toothbrush with a light mixture of water and bleach can have a good effect here, but plan to spend a long time at it. An alternative would be to regrout, particularly easy to do if the current grout is old and a surface layer can be quickly removed to leave room for new grout. Forget it if you have to remove all of the grout—it's so much work you're better off retiling.

Cleaning Bathrooms

The big problem with bathrooms is not so much dirt as mineral deposits and mildew. Fortunately, very efficient mildew and mineral (hard water) stain removers are available. You often can clean up here in a few minutes with these liquids. Keep the windows open and use a fan to get good air circulation—the fumes are strong!

A word of warning: Don't spill the strong bathroom cleaners or any bleach you may use to clean bathrooms on carpeting. They will bleach out the color, and the carpet will have to be replaced. Also, *don't* mix different kinds of cleaning agents (especially ammonia and bleach)—you could get a toxic soup with toxic fumes!

Front Doors

Don't bother to clean; slap on a new coat of paint. It will be easier, take less time, and look a whole lot better. (Note: If the surface is bad you'll need to do some cleaning. However, modern paints will cover and stick surprisingly well to many dirty surfaces.)

If the paint isn't too bad in the outer entranceway, try using a hose with a high-pressure nozzle. You can quickly remove a lot of spider webs and dirt this way.

Ceilings

If the ceiling is simply painted, then reread the paragraphs above on cleaning walls. However, many older houses have acoustical material blown onto the ceiling. Over time, this gets dirty and discolored. The worst part is that this process often happens unevenly.

If you have a dirty acoustical ceiling, you really only have two choices: You can paint it, or you can have it reblown. Reblowing can cost around $3 a square foot. Because of the expense, many people involved with fixers choose to repaint. This is probably a mistake, because when painting over an acoustical ceiling, the underlying material often absorbs huge amounts of paint. (One hint is to use shellac as a first coat.) By the time you buy dozens of gallons of paint, put it on, and redo it several times to get it right, you would probably be better off reblowing. Contact a contractor who specializes in this work. Note: You can have the surface of such a ceiling removed. However, you should check first to see if it contains asbestos. If it does, removal can be very expensive.

What Should You Paint?

We've already noted some areas should be painted and not cleaned. But in other areas, painting is almost mandatory.

The entrance, living room, dining room, kitchen, baths, and master bedroom should be painted (after the walls are patched).

New paint looks fresh and good. It's like new clothes—appealing. It will make buyers want to purchase the property.

The same holds true for the front of the house and any other side that faces the street. First impressions are critical when reselling, and nothing makes a worse first impression than dirty walls or peeling paint.

Sometimes you can get by with not painting hallways and other bedrooms if they're not too badly beaten up. You can almost always get by with not painting closets or the inside of drawers and cabinets.

Be sure you do put a nice new coat of high-gloss paint on kitchens and bathrooms, unless the existing paint is in good shape and any marks have been removed.

Should You Put in New Carpeting?

Unless the property has quality hardwood, tile, granite, or other expensive-looking floors, recarpet (unless you can clean existing, good-quality carpet, as noted above). Most people think of recarpeting, particularly of an entire house, as incredibly expensive. It isn't cheap, but it's nowhere near as expensive as you may imagine.

First, remember that when it's new, even a lower grade of modern carpeting looks terrific and will continue to look terrific for at least a year or two.

Second, installing new carpeting is much cheaper today than ten years ago, because of the new type of threads that are used (which are frequently resistant to stain and matting) as well as the many new mills that produce carpeting.

Third, in almost every major city, carpet wholesalers sell direct to the public. If you go to a carpet showroom or a department store to buy carpeting, you'll pay top dollar. But, if you buy from a wholesaler, you can often get excellent carpeting at deep discounts. Today, minimally acceptable carpeting can be installed for $15 a square yard, quite good carpeting for $25, and excellent carpeting for $35. This isn't to say that you can't pay more. You can. The sky's the limit with quality carpeting. But, for a cosmetic fixer, you can get high return for your carpeting dollar.

Select carpet in a neutral color. You want your floors to look good without causing a strong reaction. It's more likely that a nonneutral color will clash—rather than blend—with potential buyers' furniture.

Should You Install New Counters and Fixtures?

In a cosmetic fixer, often the existing countertops and fixtures such as sinks, tubs, and toilets have been damaged. If so, then you must replace them. Of course, the question remains of what quality to use. My suggestion is to make the quality match the neighborhood. If you're in a $600,000 neighborhood, don't scrimp on the fixtures and countertops. On the other hand, if you're planning to sell the house for $125,000, inexpensive solutions will do very well.

The real decisions come about when the old fixtures are merely dirty or scratched but not broken. Should you clean and fix, or should you replace?

Old porcelain tubs and sinks can be refinished without removal and, if the work is done well, they look as good as new. However, the cost of refinishing is often much more than the cost of replacing. Of course, there's also the cost of labor.

My suggestion is that you use two criteria to help you judge whether to fix or replace fixtures. First, is it difficult to get the old fixture out and a new one in so that a lot of labor cost will be involved? If so, seriously consider refinishing. Second, is the fixture old-fashioned and out-of-date? If so, consider replacing it, even if it's in good shape. Old-fashioned fixtures are a turnoff to buyers, all of whom pay special attention to kitchens and bathrooms. By the way, don't confuse old-fashioned with classic. Many brand-new sinks, tubs, and showers look like turn-of-the-century models—and are high fashion.

Unless the faucets are near new, they should be replaced. A good-looking chrome faucet assembly can be purchased for $50 or less and installed in less than an hour. It's well worth the money for the sharp look it gives.

Light fixtures fit in the same category. You want lots of light, particularly in dark corners where sunlight doesn't easily reach.

New light fixtures are very inexpensive. You can, of course, pay a fortune for some, but unless you've got an expensive house, the higher-priced models aren't really needed. Get fixtures that put out a lot of light and look good. They help dress up a property and make it much more saleable.

For countertops, the decision is tougher. It costs a lot of money to put in a nice, new tile counter. Use granite or another exotic material, and the price goes through the roof. Yet, as noted earlier, if the neighborhood warrants it, spend the bucks. Your investment will dramatically increase your chances of a sale.

On the other hand, in more modest areas, tile or even formica, will do. Or, if the existing countertops do not look bad, a grout and surface cleaning may be all that's needed.

Should Roofs Be Fixed or Replaced?

Roofs are a big-ticket expense. A good, new roof on an average-sized house can cost anywhere from $5,000 to $25,000 or more. It all depends on the type of material that you use. Often, conditions, covenants, and restrictions (CC&Rs) or homeowners' associations will dictate the minimum quality of roof that can be installed. Hence, there's a real incentive to make do with the roof that you've got.

Why not save a bundle and fix instead of replace? Look at two factors: Does the roof leak, and does it look good?

Most wood roofs will continue to look okay, even after they reach the point where they leak like sieves. On the other hand, an inexpensive composition shingle roof can look terrible yet hold out water just fine.

My own feeling is that the roof must look good for you to resell the property. Usually, the single biggest part of the property that buyers see when they drive up is the roof. If the shingles are discolored and curled, their condition diminishes the entire property's value. Therefore, my suggestion is that if the roof looks bad, fix it regardless of whether it leaks or not. But use the least expensive roofing material possible that fits in with the quality of the neighborhood. In some high-end neighborhoods that only have tile roofs, for example, you'll have to use tile. However, if every other house on the block has a composition shingle roof, why put anything better on yours?

HINT

Today, there are shingles composed of fiberglass and other materials that are quite inexpensive yet have a high-quality, three-dimensional appearance and a high fire resistance rating. I recently did a roof on a house and a detached garage made of these materials, and the entire price was only $4,700, including labor. It's something to check out.

Leaking is another matter. Most wood roofs leak. That's why tar paper or similar material is often laid underneath—to keep the water out. What this means is that, as long as the tar paper is intact, you can cosmetically fix the wood roof by inserting new shingles where the old ones have fallen out or are damaged. It's not a big chore and it ends up looking good. If you do it yourself, be careful you don't fall off the roof—it can be dangerous work.

Fixing the tar paper, on the other hand, is a different story. If you find only a couple of rips and tears here and there, it probably can be fixed fairly easily. However, if the sun has gotten to the paper and decomposed it, then it's a hopeless task. You could be patching forever, and the roof would still leak. Bad paper underneath means you need a new roof job on top.

Tile roofs, once properly installed, almost never leak until the tile breaks. After that, stopping the leaking can be very difficult, because tile roofs also use tar paper or something similar underneath to keep the water out. But, when tiles crack, their sharp edges often will perforate the tar paper beneath. You have to fix the tar paper before you can fix the tiles.

Also, if you try walking on, lifting, or moving old tiles, chances are you'll only crack more of them. For a tile roof that leaks, get an expert roofer out. An expert may be able to patch it effectively. Otherwise, you could be up for a very expensive roof job.

Should You Paint or Replace Old Stucco?

Many houses have stucco exteriors. Stucco is essentially cement and paint affixed to chicken wire; it looks good and lasts a long time.

Eventually, however, with sunlight constantly hitting it, a stucco wall will begin to look bad. At that point, you need to do something.

But experts will quickly point out that paint is actually inside the final coat of stucco. That means, they say, that you should only restucco (with new paint in the mixture), not paint. Is that true?

Technically, it is. If you want a long-lasting job, restucco, don't repaint. However, if you want a job that will look good for five or ten years, paint. I always do. Restuccoing costs thousands of dollars. I can usually get an exterior repainted for a fraction of the restuccoing cost as long as it's not too big a surface. Use latex paint; it lasts better than oil paint on stucco and is far easier to clean up.

Should You Scrape Wood Clean before Painting?

The rule book says to always scrape before repainting. The reason is obvious. If you paint over loose chips of paint, it will eventually give way and flake off, taking the new paint with it.

However, the truth is somewhat different. The reason paint flakes and chips off is often twofold. First, moisture got under the original coat of paint as it was drying and prevented it from adhering properly. The original paint may also have been cheap, hence deteriorating rapidly from weathering.

My suggestion is that, if you don't need a highly polished look, use a metal scraper to get off the loose chips. Don't strain to remove the paint that's sticking well. If it's sticking now, it'll be sticking ten years from now, as long as moisture doesn't lift it off.

Use a seal first, if possible. Then use a thick paint (some say oil is better) to cover the wood and the old strongly adhering paint. Be sure to paint the edges of the wood and not just the flat surfaces. Water gets in from the edges.

WARNING

Don't attempt to scrape, sand, or burn off old paint that contains lead. You could release lead into the atmosphere and inhale or ingest it yourself—which can be deadly. Lead-based paint was phased out in 1978, but older homes (and some younger ones) still contain it. In order to remove lead paint, you have to take the material the lead paint is on to a toxic dump site or have a lead mitigation service remove it for you—very, very expensive!

Should You Plant Your Lawn from Seed or Put in Sod?

The answer here should be fairly straightforward. For a 1,000-square-foot lawn, planting from seed costs about $20; putting in sod costs about $3,000. $20 versus $3,000? Now, which should I do?

Of course, I'm exaggerating a bit here. You do need to use more fertilizer with seed. The ground needs to be prepared for either type of lawn, but more preparation is needed for seed.

The difference is in the results. If you use good quality, fresh sod, you'll have a fabulous, thick lawn in a matter of days. If you use a good quality seed with proper ground preparation and adequate fertilizer, it will take several months to achieve a lawn that looks even remotely close to sod.

The seasons in your part of the country will also influence your choice. If possible, plant the lawn as your first order of business. That way, while you're patching, fixing, and painting, you can be watering the lawn and watching it grow. A few months later, when your main work is done, the lawn is ready.

The same holds true with shrubs and bushes. If you have the time, buy them young and small and let them grow.

Only if you don't have time—because of the season or your own timing—should you spend the extra bucks to buy shrubs and other perennials fully grown. The same is true for installing sod.

What about Air-Conditioning, Heating, and Plumbing?

These are big-ticket items, and you normally don't need to worry about them in a cosmetic fixer. I wouldn't even bother to put in a new water heater unless the old one leaks.

Remember, with a cosmetic fixer, what you want to do is to fix those things that look bad. Appearance is everything. In Chapter 14 we'll deal with the big items that are very costly to fix or replace, but which you can't easily see.

14 Solving "Impossible" Problems

Occasionally you'll run into a fixer that has a single big problem (other than environmental, which we'll cover at the end of this chapter). It could be a rejuvenator or a broken-back fixer. What counts is that something is so wrong with the property that it drives the value down and thus makes it a good candidate for your efforts.

What could such a problem be? I can recall one fixer that was more than 80 years old and was heated exclusively by fireplaces. It simply had no modern heating system of any kind. What was worse, it had a tiny crawlspace instead of a basement, so installing a furnace below was impossible. The solution was to install a forced-air furnace and central air conditioner in the attic with attic and wall ducts. The solution was relatively inexpensive.

Working around the big problem in this kind of fixer involves at least three elements: Recognition of the true problem, creativity in finding a solution, and execution in fixing it properly. We'll cover each step.

How to Recognize the Problem

You'd think that the easiest part of dealing with a big-problem fixer is recognizing the big problem. But I've found that very often that's simply not the case. Many times, the hardest part is determining exactly what the problem really is.

For example, not long ago I was looking at a property in the $300,000 range. What enticed me was that the owner was asking $50,000 less than I'd expect the property to sell for.

Now a $50,000 cut in price usually means something is significantly wrong. However, the two-story house was only about 11 years old, seemed to be in fairly good shape cosmetically speaking, and was well located in a good neighborhood. It seemed too good a deal to be true . . . and it was.

When I asked the seller why he had reduced the price, I was told, "The house has a 'cracked slab' and we want a quick sale. We're selling it strictly 'as is.'"

"Cracked Slabs"

The seller used two terms here that immediately put me on guard: cracked slab and as is.

Houses in many parts of the country are built on top of a slab of concrete. Typically, a peripheral foundation goes down 18–24 inches, but the slab itself is poured over sand and a membrane (used to keep moisture out) and is typically only 4–6 inches thick. When a slab cracks, the house on top of it can shift, leading to cracks in walls and ceilings.

The thing about slabs, however, is that they almost all crack eventually. That's why they have reinforcing steel inside them. Even if the concrete is broken, the steel holds the pieces together. Once the causative problem for the cracking (often bad water runoff) is corrected, the slab stabilizes, often for the life of the property. I've owned many properties with apparently severe slab cracking, and it hasn't been a problem. Therefore, I was not overly concerned about the cracked slab, although I certainly wanted to scrutinize it more.

"As Is" Sales

Of greater concern to me was the owner's insistence that the sale be "as is," that the owner would not warrant the property no matter what was wrong.

It's important to understand that, in today's marketplace, there really is no such thing as an "as is" sale, at least not in terms of what it used to mean. In years gone by, selling "as is" meant the buyer bought blind. The seller didn't disclose anything about the property, and the purchaser agreed not to come back at the seller with complaints after the sale, no matter what was wrong. The buyer truly was purchasing a "pig in a poke."

Today, in almost all parts of the country, sellers must disclose all known problems, even if they sell "as is." Further, buyers are entitled to an independent inspection. Then, if problems are found, negotiations follow that typically result in a lower price because of the problem. Buyers can't complain to the seller after the sale, when everything is disclosed, and in that sense property sales are "as is." But in the bigger scheme of things, because everything is presumably out in the open, buyers really aren't buying a pig in a poke, and the old meaning of "as is" is gone.

Today, only a desperate seller usually attempts to sell "as is," because those two words alert buyers that a property has a serious problem, and usually means a significant price reduction.

HINT

If you're a seller, it's usually best simply to disclose problems and warrant the property in the usual way. Attempting to sell "as is" only makes buyers wary, gives you less protection than you may think, and lowers the sales price.

Thus, when this seller told me he was selling "as is," my "be careful" antenna went up. Maybe he simply didn't realize how those words sounded. Or maybe he was foolishly trying to conceal something. Whichever way it came down, I figured it had something to do with the cracked slab, because that was the only potentially serious defect he had disclosed.

So I made my own inspection of the property. The seller was eager to point out some relatively minor cracks in the ceilings and walls of the second floor, which he said were due to the slab's cracking. There was nothing really unusual there, and the cracks were mostly cosmetic.

As we walked through the first floor, I asked him where the slab was cracked. He indicated there were a few cracks here and there, but they were under the wall-to-wall carpeting and couldn't be readily seen. If I made an offer on the property, of course, he would have the carpeting rolled back so I could look at them. Again, this was nothing unusual.

Finally, we walked into the family room, which was by the garage on one side of the property. He pointed out a bigger-than-expected crack in the wall and ceiling, and said that the slab had a separation between the family room and the rest of the house. Although the visual cracks seemed severe, again I judged that they could be cosmetically covered, as long as they didn't get worse.

Then, as I was walked out of the family room into the garage, I noticed something odd. I kept tripping over my feet, as though they weren't working properly. I paused and looked back at the family room . . . and then it struck me. The room was not level. The room had shifted so that it slanted downward on one side, as much as several inches, I guessed. The slanting was hard to see, but I could feel it with my feet. This was more than just a cracked slab.

I went back in and took a large marble out of my pocket, which I carry for just such occasions. I placed it on the floor on one side of the room. It immediately rolled to the other side, over the carpeting. That indicated a serious slope.

When I asked the seller about the problem, he said it was simply the ground "settling."

Yes, ground does tend to settle under a house after it's built. However, the settling doesn't usually all take place in one direction. This was something else.

We moved outside and I scanned the lot. It had a high slope upward in the back, the house itself was on a level site and the ground sloped downward in front. Other houses on the street were similarly situated. But there was something odd about the overall slope of the land.

When I moved to one side and tried to imagine the slope as it had been before the house was built, I immediately saw the problem. A notch had been cut out of the hillside to create the building site. However, the notch wasn't big enough to hold the whole house. So what probably had happened was that the dirt taken from the notch was dumped on the downside of the slope, thereby extending the building site out. Most of the house was built where the hillside had been notched. But the family room and garage had been built on the land that had been filled.

"Cutting and filling," as this technique is called, can work well, as long as the filled ground has been properly tamped down. This involves using special tampers or grading with heavy equipment to take all the "give" out of the soil. I guessed this had not been done. As a result, the filled area was sinking, while the notched area remained firm. In short, the house was slowly splitting in half. The cracked slab was not the problem but the symptom. And the remedy would have to be nothing less than lifting up the portion of the house that was falling, recompressing the ground, and then putting the house back.

Naturally the seller was offering a discount of $50,000. In my head I calculated that it would cost three or four times that to fix the problem, if indeed it could ever be fixed.

When I confronted the seller with my analysis, he didn't deny it, making me suspect he had known about it all along. He said that was why he had knocked $50,000 off the price. When I suggested the problem was far more serious than $50,000 could solve, he shrugged. That was all he was willing to discount.

In other words, he was waiting to hook some poor fish who would think that the cracked slab was the problem and who would buy, thinking that a few cosmetic fixes would do the job. By the time the unwary buyer found out what the real trouble was, I suspected the seller would be long gone.

All of which is to say that discovering the true problem can be the biggest part of the battle. Below are some guidelines to follow when you're looking at a house that you suspect has a big problem.

Guidelines for Finding the Big Problem

Never rely entirely on what the seller says. Sellers may disclose only part of a problem. Separate symptoms from cause. What you see may only be a symptom of a bigger problem that is not as easily visible.

Beware whenever a seller offers a property "as is." There may be a bigger, hidden problem that you're overlooking. Always inspect the property thoroughly yourself and don't jump to conclusions as you go through. Let your senses and your common sense guide you. If you don't know or aren't sure, bring in an expert. Soil engineers are good sources to inspect houses that seem to have minor cracks.

Can You Find a Creative Solution?

Assuming you've discovered the problem with the house, your next task will be to come up with a solution. However, the more creative your solution, the better the chances are that you can make more money on the deal, because creative solutions often save money, big money. In our previous example of the cut-and-fill house, I couldn't find any creative solution to save money. Fixing the place would simply have to be done the old-fashioned way and cost a fortune. However, if there had been a creative solution, perhaps I could have bought the property for the seller's asking price and still made money. Consider this true example.

Rita was an entrepreneur who was very clever with fixers. She had done several and had always managed to make a good profit. Now she was looking at a home built on a hillside near west Los Angeles. As those familiar with the area know, property values there have risen so high that even marginal lots are used for home construction. Sometimes homes seem to jut right out of the hillsides on impossible slopes. They are often subject to the perils of erosion, earthquake, and hillside fires.

This particular house had an erosion problem. It was built in a wash on a moderately steep lot. The house was on two levels going down the hillside. Over time, however, the lot had slowly eroded. With each rainfall, less of the lower end of the lot was left, until, when Rita saw it, the lower portion of the house was hanging out over space where the land originally supporting it had fallen away. The house was not on a slab but instead had a wood frame and wood floor, and the foundation beams were hanging together just by the nails in them.

Of course, the house had been condemned by the building department, and the owners had moved out. They had stopped making payments on their mortgage, and the bank had foreclosed. Now the bank was trying to sell but having a hard time of it.

Rita discovered that the bank wanted to sell for land value only, figuring the house was a total loss. They wanted $900,000 (as I said, the area was very desirable). However, the few potential buyers who had come by were skeptical. Even if they bought just for the lot, they would still incur the cost of scraping the existing house. Then they'd have the problem of dealing with the lot, which, because of the erosion that was taking place, might be unbuildable.

Enter Rita. She spent several days at the site, checking out the building. It was still solid, though cosmetically cracked in many areas. The part that was jutting out over space sagged but essentially was still all together. It just had no land foundation to hold it up.

Then Rita examined the land beneath where the house jutted out. The hillside, though not very steep, just kept on going down. There was no level site below from which she could build upward with a new foundation. It seemed hopeless.

On her drive home, however, she passed some construction work on a freeway overpass. She noticed that the workers were sinking pilings deep into the ground to stabilize the structure in a soft soil area, and a possible solution came to her: Why not drive pilings deep into the hillside to support the property?

Rita contacted a construction firm that specialized in such work, and an engineer came out to take a look. He said that the house could be supported by slamming perhaps five pilings into the mountainside. However, his firm would want $50,000 apiece just for the pilings. And then extensive steel work would be needed to connect them and build a base for the house. Plus, there would be the matter of supporting the house while the work was done. Again the situation seemed hopeless.

Rita persevered, however. She contacted a different firm and asked about driving one very long, thick piling down into the earth, then supporting the whole back end of the house on it. The engineer from this second company spent some time making calculations and said it could be done, but the total cost including the piling, the steel supports, and putting the house in place would cost around $300,000. Rita had him put his bid in writing.

Next she approached the bank and offered them $300,000 cash for the property. She planned on using another property she owned as collateral to borrow the cash. She reasoned that the bank would not want to give a loan on the lot. They would want to sell it outright and get it out of their system. But would they take her lowball offer?

The bank countered at $450,000 cash. However, Rita didn't have that much. So she offered the bank $300,000 cash and another $150,000 in six months. They accepted.

The rest was whirlwind work. Rita borrowed the money she needed for the construction work from relatives and friends and had the piling put in place. The crew did it in three weeks, then built a steel foundation from it to solid ground and placed the house on it.

Two months later, she not only had a buildable lot, but she had a fully built house on it. All that remained was to fix the cosmetic damage and resell.

The upshot of this story is that Rita sold for nearly two million dollars and cleared more than a million on the deal, all in less than six months.

How? She came up with a creative solution that no one else thought of. If the original owners had conceived of a single strong piling to hold up the house, they might have saved their property. If the bank executives had thought of it, they would have saved their company a lot of money, plus potentially made a profit. But only Rita thought of it, and the rewards went exclusively to her.

Brainstorming

Although Rita figured out the answer by herself, you and I won't always be so clever or fortunate. Often we will need some creative help from others. For that reason, I strongly suggest you consider brainstorming.

If you have a dream team (as described in Chapter 8), put the problem to them. However, be careful in your presentation. If you describe the property as a hopeless situation, others are likely to think of it that way, too. On the other hand, if you present it as a challenge with great rewards possible, your associates will put their thinking caps on and go to work.

If you don't have a dream team, then ask everyone you know and meet for help. You can describe the situation without giving the property address and thus, hopefully, not risk giving the deal away to someone who has a better idea and doesn't confide in you. Make sure to ask people in different aspects of construction. It's sort of like asking a doctor for an opinion. If you ask a foot doctor, they'll tell you to get arch supports. Ask a back doctor and you need a brace or surgery. Ask a chiropractor and you need manipulation. In the building trades, you'll get different perspectives from general contractors, engineers, and specialty contractors. The thing is, one of them may just come up with a creative solution no one else considered. And you could be on your way.

Finding the creative solution is often the answer to turning a catastrophe into an opportunity. If you can do it, you, too, can enter the ranks of those elite entrepreneurs who make handsome profits on fixers. Below are some guidelines to consider when looking for the creative solution.

Guidelines for Finding the Creative Solution

Contact experts in the field who have done the work before and can assure you that your solution will fly. Then, get them to put it in writing. The last thing you want to do is buy a property based on an idea for creatively fixing it up, only to find that your hoped-for solution was actually a pipe dream.

Try to work with expensive properties. As we've noted before, higher-priced properties offer more potential profit, particularly when one big problem needs to be solved.

When you learn that all the current thinking suggests that there's no answer, try gaining a different perspective. Brainstorm with your dream team or with anyone else who can even remotely understand the problem and pose a solution. There's simply no telling from whom you might get a workable, creative solution to your problem.

Make sure your solution is viable. The trouble with many creative answers is that they are untested. Yes, it may seem like it will work, but will it?

Can You Execute?

Success eventually comes down to execution. You can have the best property and the perfect solution, but if you can't execute, you can't make the deal. Executing means being able to buy (or at least tie up) the property, get the necessary work done—including getting all of the permits—and then resell for the anticipated profit. Fall down on any of these steps, and you could easily lose instead of make money.

Buying the Property

In the second part of this book, we discussed various methods of buying a fixer that you can apply in the vast majority of cases. However, a property with a big problem can pose special difficulties. For example, Rita could not get financing of any kind on the property she wanted to buy because of its obvious problem. Even the bank that held it as a real-estate owned property (REO) refused to finance it.

Trouble getting financing is not unusual with a big-problem property. If the house is falling down the hillside, partly burned, off its foundation because of an earthquake or a hurricane, or otherwise damaged in such a way as to be uninhabitable (the key word), chances are that no regular lender will give you a mortgage on it. If so, you need to finance it in a different fashion.

Here are four methods of irregular financing that you may want to consider for a big-problem property:

1. In our example, Rita financed the property on her own. She borrowed against another piece of property for the purchase

money price, and then borrowed from relatives for the fix-up money. While this was hard money borrowing, it also provided her with an advantage: She didn't have to take in partners and, therefore, give away any of the ultimate profits to secure the loans. If you're faced with coming up with the money yourself, don't overlook any possibilities, including equity financing on another property, credit card loans, and personal loans from friends and family.

2. Another alternative is a hard money loan from a private or institutional lender. These people loan strictly on the value of the property, regardless of condition. Be warned, however, that even they will falter when the lot itself is in trouble, as in Rita's case. Be prepared to pay very high interest rates.

3. Don't forget about real estate capital venture money, available almost everywhere. What this means, however, is that you, in effect, take in a partner. Your partner puts up the money you need. In exchange, you do two things: (a) You guarantee to repay the money no matter what ultimately happens in the deal, and (b) you agree to give your partner a percentage of the profits, if any, when the deal finishes. Sound like a rip-off? It is, but if you need the money and it's the only way you can get it . . .

   Talk to people in real estate brokerage offices, title insurance offices, and some small lenders to get names of real estate venture capitalists. They probably will know of someone who will loan on any property, for a price.

4. Take in the seller as a partner. We discussed this in detail in Chapter 11.

Getting the Work Done

We've already talked about doing the work yourself versus hiring it out. (If you're still not sure, check Chapter 15.) However, with a big-problem fixer, there's the additional difficulty of getting approval of government agencies for the work you have planned. This can be far more difficult than it may first appear.

Consider Rita's case. Houses in her area are generally built in two ways. Either there's a peripheral foundation and a slab, or there's a full foundation and a wood floor. Occasionally, the house is jacked up on piers or supports in a hillside situation. But seldom are pilings used (the kind that are sunk deep into the ground).

The problem here is that, while the building and safety department (which issues permits) knows about the usual kind of building, they don't know about the less-usual type. That means that they will be skeptical. They will want to see engineering reports. They will want reasonable explanations about how you plan to move heavy equipment in and out. They will want to be reassured about noise. In short, to get the work done, you'll need to have all your ducks in order. You must be able to answer all sorts of questions and provide massive documentation. Even then, getting approval may take months.

How Should You Deal with Neighbors?

Neighbors don't like noise, dust, mess, or confusion. They want to be able to enjoy their property in peace and quiet. When you do work, you almost certainly will cross them. So you had best be prepared for potential confrontations.

One entrepreneur I know who does a lot of fixers involving heavy construction work makes it a point to visit all the neighbors before any work begins. He introduces himself and explains that he'll be fixing up the neighboring property so that it won't be an eyesore anymore. And he explains that he'll do it as quietly and with as little mess as possible. But, he tells the neighbors, if they find the noise is too loud or there's a problem, they should come see him right away, and he'll do his best to correct it.

My friend accomplishes two things in this way. First, he introduces himself and becomes a person and a face to the neighbors, so that when things go wrong, they're likely to say, "Oh, that's Paul's house work. He's okay. It'll be over in a few days." Or, if they're really unhappy, they call *him* instead of the city, county, or police. That way, he has first chance at solving whatever the problem might be. It's something you may consider doing as well, even if your fixer job doesn't involve a great deal of noisemaking or fuss.

When you don't contact the neighbors. There is a corollary here. I once had a friend, Joey, who bought a fixer, didn't go around to meet his neighbors, and didn't bother getting a permit. Instead, he worked round the clock on his property. It didn't take long before angry neighbors complained to the city. The city discovered the work was taking place without a permit. They immediately shut Joey down. Not only did they require he get a permit, but they seemed to evaluate his plans more strictly than others. They also put stringent work times on him. In short, they hounded him until the work became a nightmare—something he could have avoided by taking the appropriate precautions early on.

Reselling and Disclosures

Presumably, by the time you get ready to resell, you've cured the problem. However, to protect yourself, you should disclose what the problem was and how you fixed it.

For example, Walter was a builder whose specialty was stabilizing houses in an area of extensive mudslides. The truth is, the homes should never have been built where they were. However, they were and thus kept sliding down hillsides and across washes every rainy season. He made a fortune buying them, fixing them up, and then reselling them.

However, when he resold, Walter told every buyer that the house had slipped, that the soil was not stable, and that he had attempted to stabilize the house in the soil. He provided highly technical engineering explanations that showed what he had done, which included forcing a special, cement-like solution into the soil and driving steel pins deep into the earth. Walter wanted to be absolutely sure that no buyers could ever come back later on, if a house slipped again, and say they hadn't been informed of the risk.

With full disclosure, however, the danger was that potential buyers would be scared away. To get around this problem, Walter offered a limited warranty. He said that if any slippage occurred within three years, he would fix it for free. If slippage occurred after three years, he would pay for two-thirds of it the fourth year, one-third the fifth, and none after that. His warranty, however, was not transferable if the buyers resold.

He never seemed to have a problem reselling. Would-be buyers seemed to feel that, if he was willing to warranty the house for three years, it would probably be there forever. Besides, most didn't plan to stay there forever but instead planned to resell themselves.

Most of his fix-ups worked fine, and the houses never slipped again. But, the soil being the way it was, a few did. I don't know how those owners handled it, but I do know that they never came back complaining to the builder.

When you resell a property that has had a major problem fixed, disclose the details. If necessary, work out a warranty program.

CAUTION

Never try to hide a problem that you fixed or how you fixed it. Yes, chances are nothing will come of it anyway, and by not mentioning it, you may secure a quicker sale. But, if by some bad luck, the next owners do discover the problem and the fix and, what's worse, find that the problem has returned, be prepared for a very unpleasant phone call. There's not much worse than being forced to pay for damages on a property you don't own anymore.

Big-problem fixers are great because they usually offer the chance at making big profits. But be careful: identify the problem, figure a way to fix it (be as creative as necessary), and execute your plan, including a safe resale. Then you can truly enjoy your rewards.

Dealing with Big Environmental Issues

In the old days, I can remember using a blowtorch to remove oil-based paint, using a spade to lift up and smash old floor tile, and wrinkling up my nose at the acrid smell of new wood paneling being installed. None of us who did this sort of thing ever thought twice about the dangers from lead, asbestos, formaldehyde, or other poisoning. The truth is, we didn't know any better.

But today, if you're going to do any kind of fixing up of houses, you'd better be keenly aware of the dangers to you. You also should know what dangers lurk in the property that must be disclosed to a tenant or seller.

Working with Lead-Based Paint

Prior to 1978, lead was a common additive to paint, particularly oil-based paint. In that year it was banned, however, and most houses built since then contain lead-free paint. I say "most," because builders were allowed to use up their existing supplies of paint, so some houses built later did contain leaded paint.

If you're working with fixers, there's an excellent chance you'll be around houses that were built prior to 1978 and that you'll need to repaint large portions of them. If so, how do you deal with the lead in the existing paint?

What's the health risk? In 1992, the secretary of the Department of Health and Human Services called lead the "number one environmental threat to the health of children in the United States."

Lead is an insidious toxin, because symptoms often appear only after a long period of exposure.

At high levels, lead can cause convulsions, coma, and death. At low levels, it can adversely affect the blood system, kidneys, central nervous system, and brain. It can cause problems such as hyperactivity, muscle and joint pain, high blood pressure, and loss of hearing.

Children and fetuses are particularly susceptible to lead poisoning, because it is more easily absorbed into growing bodies. Also, children are more likely to get lead in their systems, because they tend to put their fingers in their mouths or lick or chew on lead-coated areas such as door jambs or window sills covered with lead paint.

Removing old lead-based paints. There are two issues here. The first is your safety when removing paint with lead in it. The second is the safety of future tenants or buyers because of lead-based paint in the house. Let's first deal with removing the lead.

When you (or people working for you) attempt to remove leaded paint, it can be released into the atmosphere, causing a health problem. For example, sanding lead-based paint produces a fine dust that can easily be inhaled. Torching lead produces lead fumes that can be inhaled. Yet, these once were the two most common methods of removing old paint in a house.

One common misconception is that you can avoid lead dust by wearing a common air-filtering mask. However, lead dust is so fine that even many of the best air filters won't catch it all. For example, if you were to attempt to use a common household vacuum cleaner to sweep up lead, chances are you would simply be reintroducing it into the air. The cleaner would suck up the lead dust and dump it into its bag. But the bag (which allows air to filter through) would not catch the fine lead dust and thus would just expel it back into the air.

Furthermore, the lead itself may not be stable in the paint. The paint could be peeling, flecking, dusting, or otherwise decomposing and releasing lead into the nearby environment. Lead might be on the floor, on dirt next to outside walls, or indeed everywhere around the old paint.

Getting expert help. The best way to remove old, lead-based paint is to get expert help. Lead abatement companies are trained in the safe removal of lead-based paint. You can get more information on inspections and home risk assessments from the National Lead Information Center at 800-424-LEAD (800-424-5323) or at *www.epa.gov/lead*. The Center also can assist you in finding companies that remove lead-based paint.

However, be prepared to pay big bucks. Expert lead paint removal can cost $50,000 or more for a whole house—even more for a commercial or apartment building. Another method is to get certified yourself. You can find classes, sometimes at local junior colleges, that teach what air-filtering apparatus to use and how to safely remove old lead paint. (Be sure that any classes you take are approved by the Environmental Protection Agency [EPA]).

Finally, sometimes you can simply remove the material on which the lead paint is located. Instead of sanding down old molding, remove the molding. (Just be sure you have it properly disposed of at a toxic dump site that accepts lead-painted materials. Burning it in an open fire may be illegal.)

For tenants and buyers. When you rent or sell a residential property these days, you must disclose to the tenant or buyer whether or not you are aware of the fact that the building has lead-based paint in it. There is even a special federal form and pamphlet to use. Check with your local real estate agent who can provide it to you, usually free of charge, or search for it at *www.epa.com.*

Thus far, as a seller or landlord, you are not required to remove the lead-based paint. But, if you're aware of it, or have done any mitigation, you surely will want to disclose that fact.

Working with Asbestos

Yet another significant health problem is posed by asbestos. According to the American Lung Association, the U.S. Consumer Product Safety Commission, and the EPA, "Asbestos is a mineral fiber. It can be positively identified only with a special type of microscope. There are several types of asbestos fibers. In the past, asbestos was added to a variety of products to strengthen them and to provide heat insulation and fire resistance."

Asbestos is commonly found in:

- Roofing shingles (and siding made of asbestos cement)
- Insulation (but not the fiberglass used today)
- Textured paint and patching compounds produced prior to 1978
- Artificial ashes and embers sometimes used in gas-fired fireplaces and heaters
- Asbestos paper or cement sheets typically used on floors and walls around wood burning stoves
- Vinyl floor tiles, vinyl sheet flooring, and vinyl adhesives

- Blankets or tape typically wrapped around hot water pipes or steam pipes in older homes
- Door gaskets on oil and coal furnaces and sometimes on wood burning stoves

If you suspect asbestos, probably the best thing to do is to assume that's what it is, until an expert tells you differently.

What is the health risk? According to the American Lung Association, breathing high levels of asbestos fibers can lead to an increased risk of lung cancer, mesothelioma (a cancer of the lining of the chest and the abdominal cavity), and asbestosis (a scarring of the lungs with fibrous tissue). The risk of lung cancer and mesothelioma increases with the number of fibers inhaled. The risk of lung cancer from inhaling asbestos fibers is increased in those who smoke.

How should you work with asbestos? Unlike lead, asbestos poses little danger unless it is disturbed. Unfortunately, when you begin fixing up an older home, you are very likely to disturb any asbestos that's in place.

While encapsulating (wrapping with a protective coating) is *not* recommended for lead, it *is* sometimes recommended for asbestos. For example, if you find asbestos wrapped around a pipe and the wrapping has not been disturbed so that fibers are breaking lose, you might be able to further encapsulate that asbestos, if it's in an area that will not be further disturbed.

Asbestos in floor tiles sometimes can be handled by simply laying a new floor on top and not disturbing the existing asbestos tile floor.

One particular problem occurs with the "acoustical" ceilings found in some homes built in the 1950s and 1960s. These ceilings were blown in and may contain asbestos. It may be possible to encapsulate them with a dropped ceiling or to seal them with paint (usually preceded by a coat of shellac). Removal usually involves wetting the material and then removing it by hand using a wide, spatula-like tool.

If you must have asbestos removed from a property, experts must do the removal. This is to protect you as well as inhabitants and even neighbors from the danger of asbestos released into the air. Asbestos mitigation companies are now available in almost all communities. Their workers usually wear protective suits and helmets with self-contained air supplies while working in areas containing asbestos.

As with lead, the cost of removing asbestos from a property can be astonishingly high. Estimate your costs around $5,000 for a small floor area and increasing from there. Once removed, the asbestos must be properly disposed of at an appropriate toxic dump site. Be sure proper removal is part of your contract with the abatement company.

For tenants or buyers. As of this writing, no federal regulation requires disclosure of asbestos in a home by a seller or landlord. However, you should check these legalities when buying or selling a property.

If you plan to rent or sell a home you've fixed up, you may want to disclose any asbestos abatement work you've done (location of abatement and the method used). Such disclosure will undoubtedly make the tenant/buyer happier and could save you a lot of hassle later on if someone discovers that work was done or some asbestos remains.

Other toxic problems. Unfortunately, lead and asbestos are not the only toxins found in the home. Others include carbon monoxide (usually from faulty gas heaters or fireplaces), heating oil (seeping from storage tanks), radon gas (rising from the ground), and formaldehyde (usually from wood products used in construction).

Unlike for lead and asbestos, however, simpler remedies often are available for the other toxins. For example, a heat exchanger in a furnace may be producing carbon monoxide gas. Replace the exchanger, and you've solved the problem. A blower system can eliminate radon gas. And being careful to avoid using wood products that leak formaldehyde fumes can go a long way to avoiding that problem in your restoration work.

An Extra Cost

In this book, we've discussed making the calculations on how much to pay for a fixer. One cost we have not taken into account, however, is for toxic substance abatement. That's because it's so difficult to tell whether it will be a factor or not.

However, if toxic substances are a problem, the costs could be staggering. Therefore, it's a good idea, before fully committing to a purchase, to call in experts to determine if such problems exist. Testing for lead paint, asbestos, and other toxins can cost the buyer less than $1,000. It's well worth the price to know about these problems beforehand instead of learning later on that you can't afford to fix up the property because of all the toxins present. With a properly drawn contract, you can back out of the deal if toxic problems are found.

15 What You Can and Can't Do on Your Own

As every person who has worked on a fixer knows, if you do it yourself, you should be able to save money. Depending on the job, you may be able to do it quicker, better, and cheaper than hiring someone else. At least, that's what we all want to believe. The truth, however, may be far different.

Always ask these three questions with regard to doing the work yourself versus paying others to do it:

1. Do you know how to do the work?
2. Do you have the time (or is your time better spent elsewhere)?
3. Will doing it yourself really save you money?

You may think you know the answer to these questions and that the answer always is to do it yourself! But I would beg to differ. More often than we may realize, it turns out that having someone else do the work is quicker, easier, better, and cheaper. The example that quickly springs to mind is insulation.

Have you ever installed insulation? Most of us think that any fool can do it. You just unroll it (it usually comes in long sheets tightly wound in rolls or in flat "bats") in the attic or, if it's going into an you want it. Pushing large rolls through a tiny attic access hole is not my idea of fun. Getting scratched all over by microscopic particles of rock wool or fiberglass is not my idea of fun, either. Finally, getting it to lie down evenly everywhere is no easy feat.

I once was converting a garage to guest quarters and was putting in a bathroom and bedroom over the garage. I needed to have insulation installed on the ceilings and walls, which were all exposed and easily accessible. So I went out and priced the insulation. I found out what it would cost me at the best discount. Then, more or less just for the heck of it, I called up someone who installed insulation professionally and had them come out to give me a bid. Their price, installed, was less than my cost to buy the material alone! Guess whether I did the work or hired it out?

Can You Do as Good a Job as a Professional?

Of course, with insulation, it really doesn't matter much whether the job is just okay or really good. After all, once the wall covering is on, no one sees the work. The same applies to plumbing. Who cares if, when you sweat a joint on copper piping, it looks like Frankenstein's monster's scar? All that matters is that it holds up to water pressure. Nobody's going to see what it looks like. On the other hand, some jobs are all show. These include:

- Painting
- Plastering
- Wallpapering
- Wood finishing
- Carpet installation
- Tile installation

How well (or how poorly) you do these jobs is obvious to anyone who looks. If that person happens to be a potential buyer and the work looks terrible, you could lose your resale. Does that mean that you should hire out all of those jobs, even painting? Not necessarily. You can learn certain jobs quickly and do well enough to get by on the first or second attempt. These include painting as well as some simple plumbing and electrical work.

CAUTION

Never do plumbing, gas, or electrical work unless you're fully qualified. It's best to hire a professional for these to avoid any potential liability issue. And always have work properly inspected.

You can learn many of these tasks out of a book. And, in most cases, you know immediately if you did a good job or not. Either it leaks or it doesn't. Either the paint looks great or looks really bad. On the other hand, some jobs, such as taping and plastering wall board, require a lot of skill and training. It sounds as simple as putting mud (wallboard paste) and tape across a joint. Any child of 10 can do it, right? However, to do it correctly so that the wall is smooth and the seam doesn't show takes practice and skill. If you aren't skilled at taping and texturing, it's well worth the money to get a pro to do it. It's not just the money here. It's a matter of getting a finished job that looks good.

Do You Have the Time?

I have yet to see a fixer project without some sort of time constraint, often tied to money. You only have so much money, which translates into a certain number of months of mortgage payments before you must have the place finished and either move in or sell. It's been said over and over, and it's still true: Time is money.

Yes, you can do the plumbing work on the fixer. But if you do it, it may take a month. If you hire an expert, it may take 3 days. Can you afford to waste the extra 27 days? What about the other work you could be doing if you weren't fooling around with the plumbing?

Don't ever overlook time, or it will come back to haunt you. You only have so long to complete the work on every fixer you do. Be sure you factor in that time constraint when deciding who will do the work.

Are You Willing to Work for Free?

There's another point to consider. Your effort is worth something in terms of real money. If you don't believe that, then you could be in trouble.

Consider a friend of mine, Timmy, who does his guesstimating along these lines. Timmy looks mainly for cosmetic fixers. I've been along when he finds one, and because he thinks out loud, it's easy to follow his reasoning. It goes something like this:

"Painting all walls and ceilings. I guess I can do that."
"Putting in a new water heater. Yeah, I can do that."
"Installing a new furnace and air-conditioning. I've never done that, but what the heck, how hard can it be?
"Putting new stucco on the front and one side. It can't be that difficult to slap some cement on a wall. Okay, I'll do that."
"Roof leaks. I better put on a new roof as well. Oh what the heck, how long can it take to slap down some shingles? I'll do that, too."

You get the idea. Pretty soon, there's only one laborer on the job, Timmy. And he's pretty good. But he's not a professional painter, plumber, plasterer, or roofer. He's had some real disasters, fixers that he's worked on where he had to sell them again as fixers even after he'd done work! Nobody believed his work quality was acceptable—every buyer discounted those properties when he was trying to resell them.

Plus, it always takes Timmy longer than anticipated to do the job. He might spend nine months on a fixer, whereas I might spend three. During those nine months, however, he's making mortgage payments, paying taxes, insurance, and so on. Sometimes what he gains by doing the labor himself, he loses by paying out on holding costs.

The real problem with Timmy, of course, is his guesstimating. By never writing in a realistic figure for labor, he's always able to offer more for properties than those of us who add in accurate labor costs. Timmy does probably get more than his fair share of fixers this way. But, needless to say, Timmy has lost more money than he'd care to admit on many of his jobs, because he's attempted to do too much himself. It's important not to be a Timmy when you work on a fixer.

What Is Your Work Worth?

If your work is worth something, what is that value? How do you place a price tag on it? The temptation is to say your work's not worth much, because it's done in your spare or extra time. Yet, if you weren't working on a fixer, you could be working at some other salaried job. Or you could be relaxing in front of the TV with a good drink. Trading off those moments to relax has to be worth something, too.

So how do you calculate how much your time is worth, say on an hourly basis? Here are three methods, any of which may work for you:

1. *If you weren't working on a fixer, what could you make working for someone else at your regular job?* If you're an hourly worker, then it's easy to judge. Just figure your hourly wage, whatever it might be. If, for example, you make $25 an hour, and the job on the fixer requires three hours, then on your estimate put down $75. That's what doing it yourself will cost you. If you get a weekly or monthly salary, it's not hard to calculate your hourly wage. Just divide your weekly salary (for the moment overlooking benefits, which can be a sizable amount) by 40 hours a week or your annual pay by 2080 hours a year, the standard work schedule.

2. *What would a professional charge to do the work?* Let's say you need to install a water heater. You could call a plumber. Or you could call a handyperson. My feeling is that you should figure what it would cost to call the cheapest pro to do the job. A plumber might charge you $60 a hour or more plus travel time to and from your site. A handyperson, on the

other hand, might simply charge a flat fee, say $150, to install the same water heater. (Sometimes a plumber working on the side might be willing to do the job for the lower figure.) If installation took four hours, that's $37.50 an hour. In this case, I would figure my costs of labor at $37.50 an hour.

3. *Finally, what would you make if you took a part-time job to earn extra money instead of working on the fixer?* This is a bit trickier to figure, because part-time work that you do on the side usually doesn't pay the same as your regular work. Often, it's done piecemeal, and you may end up getting more or less an hour than for your regular job. A good way to judge is to think back to any side jobs you've recently had and use them as guides. If you haven't had any, consider what you might do as an alternative to fixing up the property. Then try to come as close to determining what your hourly wage would be. This is what you'll put down.

It doesn't matter which of the three methods you use. They are all arbitrary. The whole point, however, is to give yourself a wage for your work. By putting down a reasonable figure, you'll get a more realistic cost for fixing up the property.

In addition, should something go awry with your plans—if you get sick, you run out of time, the job's harder than you thought—you'll be able to afford to hire someone else to do the work without ruining your guesstimate. Further, should things go well, then when you ultimately resell, you will get paid what you are worth for the work you did.

Can You Reduce Your Overhead Costs?

Finally, there's the matter of overhead costs. To illustrate the point, consider the example of Jack, whom I hired a few years back to do some landscaping work on a fixer. Jack was a big guy. He and his partner were making a living working as repair people. He gave me a low bid of around $6,000 for doing some landscaping, concrete work, and fencing. I felt that he and his partner were capable of doing the job, so I hired them.

Jack wanted some money up front, to buy about half the supplies and equipment needed to get started, and I gave him $2,000. He immediately bought a pager and a cellular phone. He also bought stationery, business cards, and flyers to distribute through neighborhoods advertising his services.

When I reminded him that the money was supposed to go for the work on my fixer, he told me not to worry. He had it all under control. This was just something he needed to do to expand his business. The next day he showed up with a new pickup truck he had purchased to help move supplies to the job.

The upshot of this true story is that, within a week, Jack had spent the entire $2,000 I had given him on what might be termed overhead, items he felt were essential to doing his work but which did not directly contribute to my job. Then he came back to me looking sheepish and admitted he needed more money to buy the supplies that the original money was to go for.

I refused to give him another dime. Instead, I went out and bought the needed supplies and had them delivered. Then I gave him a week to get the job done. During the week, I bought the remainder of the supplies needed to complete the job.

Jack did the work with his partner, and the job was done in an acceptable fashion. When they came in for their pay, I told them I owed them $4,000 more. However, the supplies had cost a total of $3,600. I handed them $400 in cash and got a receipt.

Jack and his partner walked out with $200 apiece looking as though they had been struck by lightning. I remember his saying, "Only $200 bucks, for all that work!" I reminded him that he had already received $2,000 but had blown it on overhead. He nodded and said, "Oh yeah, that stuff."

I'm not suggesting that you might be as foolish as Jack. However, once you get started on a job, you may find the temptation to spend your money on items not directly related to the work almost overpowering.

For example, you might find that you need a new drill. You can get a consumer unit that will do the job for $50, or you can get a professional-quality drill for probably four times that amount. The temptation to say that you'll use it time and again and it will pay for itself many times over will be strong. But will that consumer unit suffice for all the work you do? Where will the money come from that you'll use to buy it? Will it come out of your labor costs or your materials costs? You have to weigh the consequences of spending more . . . or less.

Many savvy entrepreneurs who do fix-up work put in a figure for overhead. This includes money to spend on tools, on rental equipment, on a truck, or on whatever else they'll need. Thus, when buying tools to use on the job, they don't have any problem finding the funds.

The trouble, however, is that you're competing with others to get the house as cheaply as possible. Anything you add to your expenses reduces the price you can offer. Add 5 percent of the fix-up cost for overhead, and you've reduced the price you'll offer for the property significantly. At the same time, a competitor may be figuring no overhead or only a 1 percent charge for it and so offer a bid much better than yours.

My own feeling is that it's important to skimp as much as possible with the tools for the job. This doesn't mean always buying the consumer model drill over the professional model. If you will use the equipment over and over, the pro model will indeed be better for you.

Similarly, you may indeed need a pickup truck to haul supplies around, particularly if you'll be doing fixers on a regular basis. But do you need a new truck, or will an old, beat-up model that runs well do just the job? Again, don't be penny wise and pound foolish. Sometimes you can buy on credit or lease a new vehicle for only a few hundred dollars a month, compared to putting out capital to buy an old one for cash. Always compare costs to see what works best for you.

You may need a diamond blade tile cutter to do tile work in the kitchen and bath. You can buy one for $500, or you can rent almost the same model for $50. Unless you're planning to go into the business of laying tile, rent it.

When you need business cards and stationery, you can go to a printer and pay $150 for the finest quality, or you can use your home computer to print some of acceptable quality on your own.

Because your business is fixing up properties and not writing tomes, which should you do?

Don't let overhead bog you down. You need to spend something on tools and equipment. Just be sure it's as little as possible.

Bottom-Lining It

It all comes down to this: when you decide to tackle a fixer, you enter a highly competitive field. As in any competitive arena, the profits go to the person with the most accurate calculations.

You need to know as accurately as possible what your labor costs will be, whether you do the work or hire it out. You need to know what your cost of materials will be. And you need to know pretty darn accurately how much you'll realistically spend on overhead.

You can't do a fixer unless the seller accepts your offer, not someone else's. If a competitor offers just $500 more than you for the same property, with roughly the same deal and creditworthiness, whose offer do you think the seller will accept? Just remember, $500 may only be the cost of one piece of equipment, one hiring of a pro to do a simple job, or one botched job done by yourself.

In fixing up properties, the deals often go to the best guesstimator, because that person can make the best offer.

What's Your Fixing-up Comfort Level?

The cosmetic fixer (as discussed in Chapter 4) is what most of us feel comfortable with. We usually feel that we can easily handle painting and wallpapering. We can replace fixtures and do simple work. But we really don't want to tackle much more. At the other extreme is the builder who is confident and capable of scraping and starting from scratch.

In between is the enthusiast who is willing to tackle big jobs in older houses or work creatively to solve a difficult problem.

To help you determine what category you fall into, take the following quiz. No one has to see your answers, though you might want to compare your answers with those of any partners. There are no right or wrong answers, just answers that may help you to get a better sense of what level of fixer you can handle.

Quiz: What Level of Fixer Can You Handle?

1. Do you enjoy painting and wallpapering?
   [ ] Yes   [ ] No
2. Do you enjoy hammering, sawing, and assembling?
   [ ] Yes   [ ] No
3. Do you feel comfortable changing a wall switch?
   [ ] Yes   [ ] No
4. Have you ever installed a sink, toilet, or shower?
   [ ] Yes   [ ] No
5. Do you know how (or do you feel sure you can learn) to remove a glass frame to get a broken window repaired?
   [ ] Yes   [ ] No
6. Do you feel comfortable walking on a roof looking for leaks?
   [ ] Yes   [ ] No
7. Can you plant a garden, including lawn and shrubs?
   [ ] Yes   [ ] No
8. Could you patch and then paint the entire exterior of a home?
   [ ] Yes   [ ] No
9. If a chimney were missing a few bricks, could you cement new ones in place?
   [ ] Yes   [ ] No
10. If a backyard fence had fallen over, could you sink new posts and fix the fence?
    [ ] Yes   [ ] No
11. Are you willing to quit your regular job and risk your money on a fixer? (Perhaps a spouse could work to help out.)
    [ ] Yes   [ ] No
12. Can you install a new sink and lay tile on a kitchen counter?
    [ ] Yes   [ ] No

13. Have you ever installed or helped install a furnace? A water heater? A whole-house air-conditioner?
    [ ] Yes   [ ] No
14. If you were in the attic, would you recognize a ground wire? Would you know if the ground wire were missing?
    [ ] Yes   [ ] No
15. Could you install and populate a 200-amp circuit breaker box? (This requires professional knowledge and skills.)
    [ ] Yes   [ ] No
16. Could you work with engineers, concrete pourers, steel welders, and others to come up with a plan for stabilizing a broken foundation?
    [ ] Yes   [ ] No
17. Would you feel comfortable installing the ductwork for a furnace/air conditioner?
    [ ] Yes   [ ] No
18. Could you get building plans, steer them through building and planning departments, hire subcontractors and workers, supervise work, handle problems as they appeared, and complete a new building project?
    [ ] Yes   [ ] No
19. Are you capable of going to a lender and getting financing for a project that's only on paper?
    [ ] Yes   [ ] No
20. Do you know what a soffit, "cripple," and dormer are?
    [ ] Yes   [ ] No (A soffit is the underside of an overhang. A cripple is a short, weak wall. A dormer is a roof projection, usually with a window. If you had to read here to figure these out, mark no.)

Obviously, the more times you answer yes, the more experience and knowledge you bring to your fixers. However, just because you can't answer yes to all questions doesn't mean that you can't do all types of properties from cosmetic fixers to scrapers. It may mean, however, that you will need more time on the learning curve.

All of which is to say, just take this test with a big grain of salt. It doesn't "prove" anything about your ability to succeed. But it may show quite a bit about your current level of experience and, hence, the type of fixer personality you are right now.

Scoring: Count your yes answers:

- *20.* You're definitely a builder. You can tackle any project. But be careful about becoming involved in cosmetic fixers that are too easy, lest you quickly get bored or lose your skills.
- *15–19.* Pretty darn good. You're definitely enthusiastic about this field and, I suspect, have had some success in it along the way. You, too, could tackle just about anything, but be wary of those scrapers. You could get in over your head.
- *10–14.* You're also an enthusiast and are probably quite handy. While a cosmetic fixer would be easily within your grasp, a rejuvenator or a broken-back fixer would definitely be a challenge.
- *5–9.* Temper your enthusiasm with a touch of reality. Thus far, you're probably only a dabbler. A cosmetic fixer would suit you very well, while more challenging fixers might be a bit much just yet.
- *0–4.* There's also room for those who sit on the sidelines and cheer. Why not take a course at a local school to learn some important construction skills before plunging into the fixer business?

16 Sell Quickly for Big Profits

An old expression goes, "The proof is in the pudding." No matter what the ingredients, if it doesn't taste good, it isn't a success. Something similar holds true with fixers. No matter how little you purchase the property for, no matter how carefully you spend your time, money, and effort, if you can't sell for a healthy profit—it wasn't a successful venture.

In earlier chapters, we spoke of determining your ultimate resale price *before* you make your purchase. Presumably, you've already taken into account the important resale factors such as:

- What comparable fixed-up homes have sold for
- The condition of the local real estate market (hot, cold, or moving sideways)
- The employment market (are people out there with the means to buy?)
- The neighborhood (schools, crime rate, transportation, etc.)

As I said, the time to think of all of these was *before* you made your purchase. If you did your homework, now you're ready to find a buyer for a well-priced home. In this chapter, we'll discuss how to find that buyer quickly and efficiently so that you can take your profit.

To profit on the sale, you need to have a resale plan. Your resale plan can take several avenues. We'll consider these three:

1. Finding a buyer early in the timeline
2. Working with an agent
3. Selling by owner

How Can You Find a Buyer Early in the Timeline?

I have some friends, the Schmidts, who not only fix up properties on the side but also manage rentals for other property owners. (They have real estate licenses, usually required to run a property management firm—this is not required if you handle only your own properties.) They manage more than a hundred rental houses, condos, and apartments. In the process of managing, they talk with a great number of renters, many of whom would just love to own their own home. The Schmidts keep a list of tenants who would like to be owners and who have the savings, income, and good credit to make a purchase. When they structure a deal to buy a fixer, they often have one or more of these tenants in mind.

The Schmidts often will speak to selected tenants before and during the fix-up work. They'll bring the tenants, who may be living in anything from an apartment to a house, out to the fixer property and show them the quality of the workmanship. They try to build enthusiasm in these tenants and often succeed. Thus, by the time they are ready to sell the fixer, their buyer is ready to go.

Can you do something similar?

You, of course, probably will not manage rental property. But, if you put together a dream team as outlined in Chapter 8, at least one of your team members is likely to have some connection with rentals. Speak to that person early on and see whom they can convert from a tenant to a buyer. If you do your homework, you could have your fixer sold almost before you buy it.

Should You Be Working with an Agent?

In addition to trying to get a tenant converted to a buyer, you should structure your deal so that you're simultaneously working with one or more agents. (You can't always count on having a tenant ready to commit to a deal, so you need other options.) If you have an agent as part of your dream team, that person should be involved early on, talking up the property to other agents and looking for buyers. If you don't have an agent on your dream team (or don't have a team), then you may want to find a good agent to work with you on the resale.

Bring in this agent early on. You may want to list the property several months before it's actually finished, telling the agent that you'll be willing to sell for a little less to any buyer who commits early. Or you may want to wait until the work is finished before letting potential buyers see the project. Savvy investors who do fixers on a regular basis know they'll get top dollar if they wait until they can show off the finished home.

HINT

It's not usually a good idea to show the property prior to its being finished. Most buyers will have trouble envisioning the final product when they see the half-finished one. As a result, while you may get offers, they could be lowball offers. Some buyers may actually try to purchase your fixer as their fixer!

If you have one or two fixers to sell annually, you'll certainly want to work out a special listing agreement with an agent. You should negotiate a deep discount on the commission because of the volume of business you can offer. Keep in mind, however, that the selling agent typically only gets *half* a commission. As a result, the discount may not be as great as you hope for. On the other hand, if the listing agent also produces the buyers, then you have a *whole* commission to discount from. While some agents will not even be willing to consider a commission discount, others will be happy to do so for volume business.

Further, some real estate agencies specialize in offering discounted commissions. You'll have to decide whether one of those will be able to service your property in the way you want.

In any event, you'll want your agent on board early and talking up the property to other agents in the area. You want to use your agent's networking abilities, as these are key to finding a buyer.

Should You Sell FSBO?

Finally, you may want to structure your deal to sell for sale by owner (FSBO), without the services of an agent. If you go this route, you'll want to prepare early on. While you're fixing up, you may want at minimum to have a sign in the front yard announcing that the property is for sale. You never know who in the neighborhood may be interested and might stop by to inquire.

You also will want to allocate some time, particularly near the end of the work phase, to attempt to develop buyers. You will need time to put together a flier describing the property and post it on bulletin boards in the area. You may want to put together a short video on your property and see if the local access television channel will accept it. Local access TV often takes almost anything that people put together with a simple camcorder.

Today, selling by FSBO is greatly helped by the Internet. Virtually every property for sale (whether FSBO or by agent) is listed somewhere on the Internet. Internet listings allow potential buyers much greater freedom in finding and checking out properties than before the Internet. You can list your property early on by yourself on one of many Web sites. My two favorites are *www.owners.com* and *www.fsbo.com*. Even *www.google.com* now offers a free listing service. Some Internet sites will even allow you to list your property on the MLS (Multiple Listing Service). This is where agents list co-brokered property for sale. You can, however, expect to pay a hefty fee for this service, and as of this writing, it will probably require you to list through a local brokerage firm.

Finally, when selling the property yourself, you may need to allocate money to be spent after the work is done. If you keep the property vacant and have to wait for a buyer, you could need additional funds for:

- newspaper and other advertising;
- mortgage, tax, and insurance payments;
- utility payments; and
- maintenance, such as gardening.

HINT

Allocating post-fixer funds is often overlooked. Indeed, we don't mention it in earlier chapters when talking about necessary funds, because many people who do fixers move into the property themselves as soon as the work is done. Therefore, all of the payments mentioned above, with the exception of advertising, come under the heading of household expenses.

Some fixer investors think they can rent out the property after fix-up is complete to get revenue to pay for post-fix-up costs *and* find a buyer at the same time. Don't count on it. It's very difficult to get a tenant to do a good job of showing a property. Most are unwilling to do so because it impinges on their quiet enjoyment of the premises. Consider renting as a safety valve, but don't rent as part of your resale plan. Instead, either plan to move in yourself, or have enough time and dollars socked away to handle expenses associated with holding the property during the resale period.

The key to reselling quickly for a profit is to plan for it well in advance. Don't let the resale suddenly loom as a formidable obstacle. If you have taken it into consideration, you should have little trouble disposing of your property.

17 Get Started!

Okay, you've read this book, and now you know a lot about fixers. But so far your knowledge is all theoretical. You've got a lot of ideas, but what do you do first? How do you get started?

I can only tell you how I and how others I know got started. For most of us, getting started happened almost by accident. In my case, I was looking for a home/investment. I wanted to buy a house that I could move into and that I could resell in a few years for a profit. Along the way, I kept running into properties that needed work. It didn't take long before I put two and two together and realized I could maximize my profits by buying a fixer.

Sheila was a mortgage broker. She had occasion to learn of properties that were being taken back by lenders. She went out of her way to look at these properties, and when she found one that was particularly run down, she'd make an offer. Some of her offers were accepted.

Tom was a dentist. He made friends with some people at a title insurance company. Whenever his friends got word of a probate or trust sale, they would let him know. He would check out the property and, if it seemed appropriate, make an offer.

Bruce worked for the highway department. He subscribed to a news service (available in most communities—check with a title insurance company for its name in your area) that listed foreclosures and REOs. He checked them out.

Other people I know work closely with real estate agents. When agents learn of a potential fixer, they call up. Then it's just a matter of checking out the property and making the offer. The agents, of course, love this arrangement, because they get a quick and often easy commission.

In short, there are all kinds of avenues into the fixer field. However, the one requirement is that you must work at it. You don't have to put in 40 hours a week, or even 20 or 10. If you spend just a few hours every weekend looking at properties, within six months, you should see a great many potential fixers.

Besides, it's fun! My wife and I often make a morning or afternoon of it. We get out there and see what's available. Sellers and agents are almost always cordial. And there's the excitement of the hunt, because hardly a time goes by that we don't find at least one property with potential.

In short, what you must do is get active. A fixer isn't likely to land in your lap. You have to get out there and look for it. You have to spend some time, though not necessarily a lot of time, working at it.

My suggestion is that you pick a good neighborhood near where you live and "farm" it. Farming, in real estate parlance, is what agents do to get listings. They pick a neighborhood and then send out flyers, go door-to-door, make calls, and do whatever else they can think of to become known to the residents. In the long run, they hope their efforts will generate many listings for them. The neighborhood becomes their listing farm.

Do the same thing with fixers. Pick a nearby geographical area. (You don't want to travel long distances to work on your fixer.) Get to know your area like the proverbial back of your hand. Get to know the streets where the older properties are, the newer tract homes with problems, the streets where water erosion or flooding sometimes take place. Get to know those locations where fixers are likely to occur and become familiar with their typical problems.

Also, get to know the agents in the area. Go out with them and be sure they understand that you're ready to move if they find something suitable. You may not get a call from an agent for months, but then suddenly one will be on the line with a great opportunity property.

Get to know lenders in your area as well. There's no reason you can't drop in and ask to see the person who handles real estate owned properties (REOs). I do it all the time. In large institutions, I'm usually referred to a central office. In smaller ones, I sometimes end up talking to the bank president.

The bottom line, to reiterate, is to get active. Take a little time and make the small effort required. Touch enough bases, and you'll score!

The 15 Golden Rules for Finding, Buying, and Fixing Properties

1. *Never overpay.* Better to lose five maybe good deals than to purchase one bad one.
2. *Buy the highest-value fixer you can find.* It won't cost much more to fix up a high-end than a lower-priced house, but you'll have a bigger budget to work with and more profit when you resell.
3. *"Farm" nearby neighborhoods.* Let owners of potential fixers know you're looking. When they decide to sell, they'll call you first to avoid paying agent commissions.
4. *Mine broker listings for overlooked properties.* Look for houses that haven't sold for a long time and have poor curb appeal, those that most buyers shun.
5. *Make offers to lenders.* Get them to sell you their REOs—foreclosed properties they want to get off their books.
6. *Work the foreclosures.* Get to homeowners before the lenders take over.
7. *Avoid toxic properties.* Beware of properties with serious lead, asbestos, or other environmental problems.
8. *Put together a team of experts.* Get electricians, plumbers, agents, loan brokers, and others working with you.
9. *Make successful lowball offers.* Learn the techniques that will motivate sellers to see things realistically.

10. *Get complete financing.* Arrange for mortgages and short-term loans in advance of need.
11. *Get sellers to finance your deal.* You don't need to put up your cash, and the seller keeps more money from the sale.
12. *Put in your own seed money.* Never appear needy to anyone with whom you deal.
13. *Learn how to guesstimate.* Beat out your competition for the lowest-priced properties by correctly estimating fix-up costs on the fly.
14. *Know the difference between cosmetic and serious problems.* Never think a little paint and plaster will fix a broken foundation.
15. *Move up to apartment and commercial buildings.* Learn to fix bigger projects for bigger profits.

Index

Share the message!

Bulk discounts
Discounts start at only 10 copies and range from 30% to 55% off retail price based on quantity.

Custom publishing
Private label a cover with your organization's name and logo. Or, tailor information to your needs with a custom pamphlet that highlights specific chapters.

Ancillaries
Workshop outlines, videos, and other products are available on select titles.

Dynamic speakers
Engaging authors are available to share their expertise and insight at your event.

Call Kaplan Publishing Corporate Sales at 1-800-621-9621, ext. 4444, or e-mail kaplanpubsales@kaplan.com

PUBLISHING